Education 16-19

D1348173

The 16-19 sector of education is a transition stage for students and a system in transition for educators. This book considers the needs of older teenage students and the various forms of provision made for them. At a time of rapid change the author assesses the significance of current trends and recent legislation – for managers, teachers and lecturers in schools and colleges catering for the 16-19 age group.

Eric Macfarlane argues that the 16-19 sector provides both a microcosm and intensification of the tensions, divisions and conflicting aims and objectives present throughout the education system as a whole. He explores the differences that exist between the academic and vocational routes to qualification, between the comprehensive, selective and independent systems and between 'traditional' and 'progressive' approaches to the learning process. The ideologies and policies that have produced the present system are traced and the case for reform examined. Different management tasks in 16-19 education are considered, with emphasis on current changes in strategies and structures.

The book highlights the distinctive features of the various types of institution that provide for students aged 16-19 and the ways in which these distinctions are becoming blurred. The final chapters consider the future of 16-19 provision and the particular impact of the 1992 Further and Higher Education Act.

Eric Macfarlane is a manager and evaluator of change in education, currently working for the Enterprise in Higher Education project at Surrey University. He has extensive experience as a teacher, education officer, head and college principal. He is particularly well known as an innovator in the 16-19 field and lectures widely on this sector of education.

Educational management series
Edited by Cyril Poster

Education 16–19

In transition

Eric Macfarlane

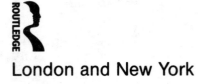

London and New York

First published 1993
by Routledge
11 New Fetter Lane, London EC4P 4EE

Simultaneously published in the USA and Canada
by Routledge
a division of Routledge, Chapman and Hall Inc.
29 West 35th Street, New York, NY 10001

Typeset in 10 on 12 point Baskerville by Witwell Ltd, Southport
Printed and bound in Great Britain by
Biddles Ltd, Guildford and King's Lynn

British Library Cataloguing in Publication Data
A catalogue record for this title is available from the British Library.

Library of Congress Cataloging in Publication Data
Macfarlane, Eric, 1931–
    Education 16–19: in transition/Eric Macfarlane.
        p. cm.—(Educational management series)
    Includes bibliographical references (p.).
    ISBN 0-415-08085-1.—ISBN 0-415-08086-X (pbk.)
    1. Post-compulsory education—Great Britain.   2. Curriculum
change—Great Britain.   3. Education and state—Great Britain.
    4. Education, Higher—Great Britain.   I. Title.   II. Title:
Education sixteen–nineteen.   III. Series.
LC1039.8.G7M33   1993
378.41—dc20   92-24739
                                                                      CIP

Contents

This book is dedicated to all who seek to improve the quality of learning in schools and colleges and particularly to those who strive to make local sense of national confusion in the 16–19 sector.

Figures

Foreword

There are few educationists in the UK with the breadth and depth of experience in the field of education for the 16–19 age group of the author of this book, Eric Macfarlane. He was from its foundation the principal of Queen Mary's College, Basingstoke, one of the first of the sixth form colleges to be established in England and a prototype for a generation of such institutions within Hampshire and beyond. Most recently he has been using his extensive knowledge of 16–19 institutions – tertiary colleges as well as sixth form colleges – to survey the whole field of educational provision for this age range.

The book has proved to be even more timely than when it was originally commissioned for the Routledge Educational Management series. Recent legislation, most particularly that which took these institutions out of the financial control of Local Education Authorities and created uniform conditions in what was once a morass of conflicting regulations, has made the book essential reading for administrators, all staff within 16–19 institutions and those responsible for advising 16-year-old pupils about their future education, teachers and parents alike. It has its messages too for overseas readers, where similar developments are either currently taking place or are under consideration. Eminently readable, this book is an invaluable critique of a vital development in British education.

Cyril Poster
Series editor

Introduction

16-19: A SYSTEM IN TRANSITION

In recent years education has moved to the top of the political agenda and become the subject of constant public debate. The Education Reform Act of 1988 has led to the most extensive changes to our system of compulsory schooling since 1944. Four years later the 1992 Further and Higher Education Act introduced another set of major reforms, this time for the Further Education (FE) and Higher Education (HE) sectors. The changes envisaged for 16-19 provision are particularly significant and far-reaching.

Successive governments have shied away from developing a clear policy for the 16-19 age group. This part of educational provision is bewilderingly complex, offering, in theory, wide-ranging variety of opportunity, but in practice often arbitrarily assigning young people to a narrowly specific educational experience. The 16-19 sector provides a microcosm of the tensions, inequalities, conflicting ideologies and confused aims and objectives present in the education system as a whole.

Education for the 16-19 group is characterised by deep divisions symptomatic of the society in which we live, divisions between the private and public sectors, the academic and vocational routes to qualification, selective and non-selective systems, and 'traditional' and 'progressive' methods of course delivery and approaches to learning. The 16-19 curriculum has for thirty years been the subject of repeated scrutiny, surveys and recommendations for reform; yet we have still to provide students with an effective balance in their studies between breadth and depth, theory and practice, content and process, knowledge and skills. As a nation we are undecided over whether those aged 16–19 are pupils who require the security of a school community, or students who thrive in a fully adult college environment, or, indeed, whether they are best catered for in an institution designed specifically for their transitional stage of development.

In the last twenty-five years Local Education Authorities (LEAs) have responded in various ways to the need to provide for the full ability range of post-16 students. Sixth form and tertiary colleges have provided a broader curriculum and a new style of educational environment for the 16–19 age group. School sixth forms and FE colleges have undergone a change of character. Greater flexibility and imagination are evident in the organisation and management of institutions as they alter their structures and systems in response to student needs.

The 16–19 curriculum is also changing. Vocational courses, in particular, are being modernised and upgraded in order to deliver a wide range of skills and competences required by today's employers. Whilst much of the academic 16–19 curriculum remains rooted in the past, an increasing number of students are benefiting from newly-designed syllabuses. Modular approaches have shown how students can be given a broader range of options, including the opportunity to cross the academic/vocational divide. Methods of assessment, recording achievement and reporting are gradually becoming more varied and imaginative. All these developments are beginning to make further education more relevant, attractive and accessible to school leavers.

Educational reformers have always sought an improved education system for its intrinsic merit. They are, in this instance, strengthened by the large body of informed opinion expressing concern that our future economic strength and prosperity are threatened by our failure to educate and train anything like as many of our young people as our main competitors. A succession of reports appeared in 1989 – from the Confederation of British Industry (CBI), the Royal Society of Arts (RSA), the Institute of Manpower Studies (IMS) and Manchester University – all conveying the same urgent message:

> The supply of educated people is critical to the UK's future vitality and prosperity. We are well behind our international competitors. Far too few pupils stay in full-time education

beyond the age of 16: far too few students enter higher education. Unless we change that, we cannot hope to achieve our objective: a better educated society at all levels.

(Coldstream, 1989)

	16 years	16–18 years
Australia	73	51
Belgium	92	82
Canada	92	75
Denmark	89	73
France	80	69
Germany (1988)	71	49
Italy (1982)	54	47
Japan	92	77
Netherlands	93	77
Spain	65	50
Sweden (1985)	91	76
United Kingdom*	50	35
USA	95	80

Figure I.1 Participation of 16–18-year-olds in full-time education and training, as a percentage of the age group, 1987
Note: *The United Kingdom figures include estimates of private sector further and higher education
Source: Education Statistics for the United Kingdom (DES, 1991)

Most of the 1989 reports drew attention to the demographic trends in England and Wales, which showed a sharp decline in the number of 18-year-olds - by 32 per cent from 1983 to 1995. Already this was having the effect of increasing competition for school leavers between employers and further and higher education. Another recurring theme was the approach of more open competition within the European Community (EC) and this country's inadequate preparation for that situation.

The 1992 Further and Higher Education Act was a direct response to these pressures. Its primary intention was to stimulate more young people to engage in further education and training and to aspire to higher levels of attainment. It included measures to heighten students' awareness of the world of work, of vocational courses and of employment opportunities. The need to broaden the base of 16–19 programmes of study was recognised and in particular for more students to include a vocational component in their course.

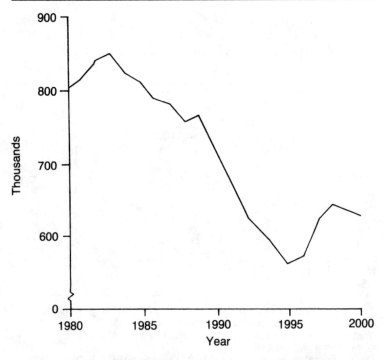

Figure I.2 Eighteen-year-old population in England and Wales
Source: Office of Population Censuses and Surveys, mid-year estimates and
(1989-based) population projections

In keeping with the government's commitment to private
enterprise, the strategy to achieve these ends was to give institutions greater freedom and flexibility to respond competitively to
market forces. The Act also took another major step towards the
removal of education from local government control: following
the 1988 incorporation of polytechnics and colleges of higher
education, all sixth form, tertiary and further education colleges
are to become free-standing, centrally-funded corporations.

There is no doubting the government's commitment to radical
change of the educational system: both the 1988 and 1992 Acts
break new ground in their strategies for taking educational
reform out of the hands of educationists and driving the system
in accordance with the economic principles of the market place.
The government's 16-19 policies, however, contain some notable
inconsistencies, particularly with respect to the curriculum and
the extent to which it needs changing. Government rhetoric on

meeting the country's needs implies sweeping curricular change at 16-19: spirited defence of the traditional A level system suggests that only vocational courses need to be reformed.

Underlying this apparent ambivalence is an internal power struggle between two government departments and their ministers. The Department of Employment (DoE) has done much, particularly through its Technical and Vocational Education Initiative (TVEI) and Enterprise in Higher Education (EHE) project, to support and encourage the view that all post-16 students should follow a broad curriculum offering an appropriate balance between content and process and between academic and vocational experiences. The Department for Education (DFE), previously the Department of Education and Science (DES), has resented the DoE's developing influence in education and has sought to retain the purity of the academic curriculum, particularly that of the traditional A level system. Thus, whilst all the national bodies responsible for education and training have been cooperating to devise ways of bringing academic and vocational curricula together, the DFE/DES has consistently pursued measures to ensure that they remain apart.

Such clashes of interest and ideology help to explain why 16-19 curricular reform is proving such a long and difficult process. They are just one example of the conflicts and struggles that are an inevitable part of managing change. The 16-19 sector of education is a system in transition. As such, it is full of tensions between new ideas and conventional wisdom, between those seeking reform and those committed to the established order. It is easy to categorise the protagonists in these struggles, the heroes and villains of the piece. It is sometimes more difficult to analyse the ambivalence of many who are caught up in the process of change. Even the strongest advocates of reform may succumb to expediency and an occasional reluctance to abandon tried and trusted methods.

16-19: AN AGE GROUP IN TRANSITION

Those who work with older teenagers have always, in one sense, been managers of change. The 16-19 group comprises a stage of human development that teenagers mostly enter as children and leave as adults. Their teachers have to be constantly sensitive to the changes involved in this rapid process of development and, more particularly, to the pace at which different individuals cope with them.

By the time that they enter college or the sixth form some students are already enjoying a range of adult experiences: they have a busy social life, they are sexually active, they are significantly increasing their spending power with wages from evening and weekend employment. They are looking for ways of expressing their individuality and their independence of adults, and their parents in particular. They smoke, drink, ride motorcycles and are impatient to learn to drive and become car owners. Others have had a premature introduction to less enviable adult experiences in homes where death, illness, parental separation or divorce have required of girls, especially, a major care responsibility for a parent or younger brothers and sisters.

All experience is a context for learning and self-development, a resource upon which the imaginative teacher will try to build and capitalise. Among the attractions of teaching the 16–19 age group are its members' growing awareness and experience of the adult world, the developing confidence and maturity that they bring to the learning process, and their desire to be involved actively in the decision-making that affects their life choices.

At the same time, students of this age are young in their experience of adult freedoms and responsibilities. Inevitably they make mistakes and need guidance. There are particular problems over ordering priorities and organising time as their lives become more complex and sophisticated. 'Mature', that is fully adult, students, with their greater experience, are often better able to cope with the dual demands of study and adult life. They are also less subject to pressure, for example from teachers and parents, to achieve examination success.

Against the undoubted dilemma of the student who seeks full recognition as an adult at the earliest opportunity has to be set the fact that many of the 16–19 age group make a slow, almost imperceptible, entry into adulthood. These are young people who make little immediate response to the challenges and opportunities offered by their changing status in law at 16, 17 and even 18. Perhaps they are absorbed in their work, or other individual interests, or keen sportsmen and women engaged in regular training, or musicians committed to daily practise. For whatever reason, they are disinclined, or simply not available, to join the social round or to undertake the wage earning that is usually required to support it.

From the security of a protective home background some students pass through their final teenage years with few major changes to their lifestyle. Unconcerned, at this stage, about exerting their individuality, they neither rebel against the home nor question the educational system of which they are a part. They may have given very little thought to the options of employment and further education at 16, simply drifting into full-time voluntary education with their peers, fulfilling parental expectations and teachers' assumptions.

These categories of young people are, of course, the two extremes, the one claiming, or unable to avoid, a range of adult experiences at 16 or 17; the other content to let adult freedoms and responsibilities wait for a while. The rest of the age group comes somewhere in between, all of them individuals developing and maturing at different rates and in different ways. Their transition from childhood to adulthood is frequently uneven and confused: their naivety and vulnerability are often evident, but at times their street wisdom and common sense surprise us. The variations of maturity within the age group, and within the individuals that comprise it, are often bewildering. They help to explain our ambivalence to students of 16–19 and our inability as a nation to agree on the best way to educate them.

Chapter 1

The sixth form tradition

THE PUBLIC SCHOOL SIXTH FORM

The sixth form originated in that most English of institutions, the public school, a source that can be detected in many modern versions of school-based 16–19 provision today.

The public school system, as we know it, dates back only to the nineteenth century, although some of its best-known examples were founded over 400 years ago. The nineteenth-century public schools were designed to produce an administrative, political and social elite and provided an exclusive way of life for the children of the ruling class. Their present-day successors number 233 with a sixth form population of 48,000.

Public schools are defined, and strengthened in their common purpose, by membership of the Headmasters' Conference (HMC), an association founded in 1869. Eligibility depends first and foremost on the size and academic quality of the sixth form. Members' schools must maintain a sixth form that comprises at least 25 per cent of their total school population and the number of sixth formers gaining two or more A levels each year must not fall below 10 per cent of the number of pupils on roll. These criteria reflect the overriding importance of the sixth form to the public schools and the extent to which the system is geared to the acquisition of academic qualifications that meet university entrance requirements.

The majority of HMC schools have sixth forms well in excess of the minimum size prescribed by the Conference, and the public school sixth form represents a much larger proportion of the school community than in the maintained sector. This is mainly because the sixth form is actually the fourth, not the sixth, year of attendance, pupils normally being admitted to a public school at 13 instead of 11 as in the maintained secondary school. In addition, the highly selective nature of the public schools means that their staying-on rate at 16 is considerably higher than that of most maintained schools. There are also a growing number of admissions to public school sixth forms from other schools.

Ultimately a public school is judged by the academic achievements of its sixth formers and, more specifically, by the number that proceed to university each year. Oxford and Cambridge places are the supreme prizes in this highly competitive academic world and the goal to which the most successful pupils strive. 'League' tables are published for both A level pass rates and Oxbridge places, and schools attach great importance to their annual position.

Academic rigour remains the key feature of the public schools. The following expectations of entrants to the sixth form are not untypical of the most selective schools:

> In order to be able to respond to the intellectual demands of an A level course with a realistic possibility of success, a student should generally, in our experience, achieve a grade A in the subject (or subjects) most closely related at GCSE.
>
> (Bolton School, 1991)

A change that is having a profound effect on the ethos of the public school system is the transition to coeducation. In 1968 Marlborough College took the radical step of introducing a small number of girls to its sixth form. This practice has become widespread and 60 per cent of the public schools now admit girls to the sixth. Numbers are increasing and a fifth of the public schools' 48,000 sixth formers are girls. In recent years a significant number of the public schools have taken the decision to become coeducational throughout and 82 of the 233 HMC schools now admit girls at 13.

The public schools are pacesetters for a much larger number of fee-paying schools that are not members of the Headmasters' Conference. The independent sector as a whole contains 952 secondary schools with sixth forms, and their 77,000 sixth formers represent 20 per cent of the country's total sixth form population. These independent schools vary greatly in size, reputation and quality. Some have very small sixth forms that can offer only a limited range of courses. However, they also include a number of famous girls' schools that call themselves public schools and meet the membership qualifications of the HMC in terms of the size and academic standards of their sixth forms. The only obstacle to their membership of the conference is the prejudice that debars women from a traditionally all-male preserve.

During the last decade, the independent sector has increased its share of the school age population from 6 per cent to almost 7.5 per cent. This growth owes much to the government's Assisted Places scheme which permits able boys and girls from low-income families to apply for independent school places with remission of fees according to a scale of parental income. For many years a number of children from the lower socio-economic groups have had a route into the independent sector by winning scholarships paid for from benefactors' endowments and legacies. With society's growing preference for meritocrats to aristocrats, such opportunities have increased. A total of 68,000 pupils in independent schools receive a contribution to their fees from such sources; another 7,500 have their fees paid, wholly or in part, by LEAs, and 30,000 assisted places are currently funded by the government.

THE GRAMMAR SCHOOL SIXTH FORM

Historically, the main link between the independent system and the government-maintained sector of education is the local authority grammar school. The name 'grammar' was first applied to some very early versions of the public school and is retained by a number of their present-day successors, notably Manchester and Bristol. The maintained grammar schools originated in those independently endowed schools which, following the 1902 Education Act, began to accept funds and a degree of control from the education sub-committee of county, county borough and urban district councils. The proportion of the cost of running these schools that was met from the rates steadily increased. Meanwhile, a number of purpose-built 'county' grammar schools were opened and maintained by councils with the help of fees paid by the parents of the children attending them. Between the two world wars free places became an increasing feature of these county grammar schools and in 1944 all fees were abolished. From then on the county grammar schools became fully state-operated and financed.

The grammar schools provided a seven-year programme of academic work, assuming that pupils would proceed to the sixth form more or less as a matter of course. In providing such an opportunity for working- and middle-class children the government was in effect taking a significant step towards recognising a state obligation to provide further education for all. At the time, though, the intention was to provide only for able children, to select a meritocratic minority whose intelligence gave them the right to enjoy similar opportunities to those whose parents paid for privileged treatment. Selection took place at 11 by means of examination. Like its 13+ public school counterpart, the '11+', as the exam became known, was designed to distinguish those pupils – girls and boys – who would eventually be capable of sixth form work and probably, beyond that, a course in higher education.

In practice the staying-on rate at 16 was much lower in the grammar schools than in the public schools. Some pupils failed the 16+ examinations hurdle; others, although academically successful, could not be persuaded to continue with full-time education. The latter were often first-generation grammar school pupils whose parents saw little point in their undergoing further years of schooling when they could be contributing to the family income. Ten years after the abolition of fee paying in maintained schools, a Ministry of Education report showed that it was unusual for more than one-third of the highly selected pupils of a grammar school – that is, 6 to 7 per cent of the age group – to proceed to the sixth form. During the next ten years, however, sixth form numbers doubled and by the mid-1960s 'staying on' had become the grammar school as well as the public school norm.

The increasing attractiveness of education after the statutory leaving age contributed to a growing dissatisfaction with the grammar schools' exclusiveness and the well-publicised unfairness of the 11+ selection process. Secondary modern schools had been introduced by the 1944 Education Act to provide a four-year general and practical course for those children – the large majority – who failed the 11+. These schools began, however, to develop 'academic streams' whose pupils stayed on beyond the school-leaving age of 15 to take the same examinations at 16 as their grammar school peers. Some of the most successful pupils then sought and gained entry to grammar school sixth forms whilst a number of secondary modern schools began to develop their own small sixth forms.

By the 1950s a number of LEAs had introduced comprehensive schools, in which the primary school practice of educating children of all abilities in the same institution was extended to the secondary sector. In 1965 the Labour government called upon all authorities to submit plans for abolishing 11+ selection and establishing a comprehensive secondary school system. Although some LEAs persistently resisted this move, the majority responded, either immediately or over a period of time, and since 1986 over 92 per cent – 98 per cent in Wales – of secondary school children in the maintained sector have been educated in comprehensive schools.

A hundred and fifty grammar schools survived the widespread secondary reorganisation of the 1970s and 1980s. The lengthy defence of their selective status has sharpened the focus of their central academic function. One of the strongest arguments in favour of selection was that the grammar school was the best means of challenging the public schools' supremacy in the education of the country's potential leaders and rulers. Thus the surviving grammar schools have a strong commitment to the traditional values and academic standards of the best public schools. This is seen particularly in their sixth forms, where there is an intense concentration on advanced level work and preparation for university entrance. Less interest is shown in the alternative forms of provision that were becoming features of grammar school sixth forms before the advent of the comprehensive. A mark of the grammar schools' success in challenging the public schools' academic achievements has been the acceptance of seventeen of their headmasters by the Headmasters' Conference – special membership granted 'in recognition of their schools' outstanding academic achievements'.

THE COMPREHENSIVE SCHOOL SIXTH FORM

The debate on the respective merits of the selective and comprehensive systems of secondary education has been much influenced by the needs of the 16–19 age group. On the one hand, the widely accepted requirement for post-16 education to be made available to a much wider ability range strengthened the case for comprehensive schools. On the other, a major problem for the comprehensive system has been to demonstrate that an all-ability school can offer its ablest pupils the same sixth form opportunities as the grammar schools and so preserve the maintained sector's challenge to the public schools.

A system that brings together all the able pupils from a sizeable area into one institution produces a large and competitive sixth form able to offer advanced level work in many different academic subjects. In the comprehensive system, with the able pupils spread round all the schools in an area, it becomes more difficult to maintain a wide range of viable sixth form courses. With the establishment in 1980 of parents' right to choose their child's school in a non-selective system, wide variations have emerged in the popularity of schools and hence the size of their sixth forms.

Within the same local authority some comprehensive schools may be able to maintain a sixth form of a size comparable with that of the grammar school, whilst others have only a handful of students engaged in advanced level work. In the inner cities, where there are often striking differences between neighbouring residential areas and between the socio-economic groups that inhabit them, the contrast is even more marked. In extreme cases market forces have concentrated almost all the able sixth formers in one or two establishments and completely denuded some schools of an academic sixth form.

Numerous strategies have been employed to enable the comprehensive system to produce viable academic sixth forms. Many of the early LEA comprehensive schemes sought to solve the problem by developing very large 11–18 schools with ten or twelve forms of entry. Even with a staying-on rate of less than 20 per cent, these schools could produce a sixth form of a size approaching that of a medium-sized grammar school. However, the institutions of 2000+ that resulted from this strategy quickly lost favour because of the complex problems of organisation and social control that many of them experienced.

An alternative to the very large 11–18 comprehensive is the upper school – the 14–18 linked with high schools and the 13–18 linked with middle schools. With an age range more akin to that of the public schools, upper schools produce a viable sixth form from a smaller community. Another strategy is the consortium arrangement whereby a group of schools with small sixth forms agree to specialise in different areas of the curriculum: students' sixth form base is then determined by their choice of advanced level studies.

Essential as it has been for comprehensive school sixth forms to establish the credibility of advanced level work, another significant challenge has been to develop a sufficiently diversified programme for a mixed-ability intake. From their inception, comprehensive schools have applied the non-selective principle at 16+ as well as at 11+, rejecting the idea of a sixth form confined to academically-inclined students following a full programme of advanced level work. Many comprehensive school pupils therefore stay on at 16 to take just one or two A level subjects whilst others enter the sixth form to improve their GCSE qualifications or, increasingly, for one-year vocational courses (for example, in business studies/office skills). None of these categories of student was unknown to the grammar school sixth form, but the comprehensive schools have greatly increased their number and extended the range of abilities entering the sixth form. Many comprehensive school sixth forms admit as many students to one-year courses as to two-year advanced level programmes.

THE SIXTH FORM COLLEGE

One of the options offered to LEAs by the government when the comprehensive system became national policy in 1965 was to separate sixth form education from the secondary school by transferring all sixth formers in a given area to one or more sixth form colleges. Two alternative concepts of such a college were offered, the one making entry 'dependent upon the satisfaction of certain conditions (e.g. five passes at O level or a declared intention of preparing for A level)', the other 'catering for the educational needs of all young people staying on at school beyond the age of 16' (DES, 1965).

This idea was not new. In 1943 the Sheffield Education Committee had considered centralising its sixth form provision in order to protect undersubscribed subjects in its nine grammar schools. In 1954 the Croydon Education Committee received detailed proposals from its Chief Education Officer, Rupert Wearing King, for a similar rationalisation of Croydon's sixth forms. In an accompanying report the CEO drew attention to the extremely uneconomic nature of Croydon's sixth form provision and the lack of stimulus for students being taught in very small groups. As with so much early thinking on the maintained school sixth form, Rupert Wearing King's concern was for the effectiveness of the Croydon grammar schools' challenge to the public schools:

> My first interest is in the pupils who are looking forward to a university, or a comparable higher education, chiefly because I am sure that it is here that the state educational system does least well in comparison with the big independent schools.
>
> (Wearing King, 1968:7)

Neither the Sheffield nor the Croydon proposals were accepted and it fell to the independent sector to provide the first examples of academic sixth form colleges in action. In 1953 Welbeck College was opened in Nottinghamshire to provide a two-year A level science education to prepare boys for officer training in the technical corps of the army. In 1962, the United World College of the Atlantic was founded at St Donat's Castle in South Glamorgan, the first of a number of international colleges to be established throughout the world. Atlantic College, as it became known, offered a two-year pre-university course to selected boys and girls of high academic ability and different nationalities.

The other quite different view of the sixth form college – the comprehensive or open-access college concept – stemmed from an awareness that the grammar school sixth form had never been as homogeneous as it usually portrayed itself and from a conviction that the sixth form of the future would have to have a much broader curricular base. It was this vision that produced the first sixth form college in the maintained sector. Mexborough Sixth Form College opened in 1965, the brainchild of Alec (later Sir Alec) Clegg, CEO for the West Riding of Yorkshire, and George Shield, the Head of Mexborough Grammar School. The college was in fact a large sixth form centre on the site of a grammar school. There were 300 students drawn partly from the school's own fifth year but also from a number of secondary modern schools in the area. The curriculum provided different levels of work with considerable choice of levels and subject combinations.

Other colleges were in the pipeline. In 1966 the new County

Borough of Luton merged the sixth forms of the boys' and girls' grammar schools to form Luton Sixth Form College. As with the sixth forms of the two grammar schools from which it evolved, admission to the new college was gained by the acquisition of O level passes in four subjects. The following year three sixth form colleges were opened in Southampton on the sites of the city's three grammar schools, all of which had large sixth forms with a well-established pattern of 16+ transfer from other schools. The Southampton Grammar School for Girls, in particular, had in 1964 stopped requiring the usual academic qualifications for entry to the sixth form – in recognition of the changing needs of students wishing to continue with their education beyond the fifth form. The LEA decided therefore that local circumstances favoured a form of secondary reorganisation that concentrated sixth form provision in 'open access' sixth form colleges separated from schools. Subsequent sixth form colleges nearly all followed this pattern and Luton became 'open-access' in 1971.

By 1992 there were 117 sixth form colleges, accommodating 85,000 students – a quarter of the country's total sixth form population. The colleges range in size from 300 students to over 1,500, but the majority have between 600 and 800 on roll. They are spread throughout the country but with a heavy concentration in Hampshire (10), Cleveland (9) and Surrey (7).

As the concept of the comprehensive sixth form has gained widespread acceptance, the sixth form colleges have taken advantage of their size to diversify their provision and to offer places to all abilities, including in several instances young people from special schools. At the same time they have been very mindful of the academic traditions of the sixth form and set great store by their extensive range of A level options. An Association of Principals of Sixth Form Colleges (APVIC) promotes the sixth form college concept, publicising their high examination pass rates and other achievements.

Chapter 2

The further education tradition

EARLY TECHNICAL EDUCATION

Technical education in Britain has a history spanning almost 200 years, although the rate of its development during that time has been uneven. The growth of the factory system produced a desire towards the end of the eighteenth century for greater technical knowledge and skill at all levels of society. Individual initiatives to meet this need led to the foundation of a number of institutions which were the forerunners of the nineteenth-century Mechanics Institute Movement.

The first such institute was founded in London in 1823 by George Birkbeck who, as Professor of Natural Philosophy and Chemistry at Anderson's Institution in Glasgow, had pioneered classes for working men and intelligent artisans who wished to know something of the scientific principles underlying their trades. By 1850 there were 610 institutes throughout the country with a membership of over half a million. The original institute in London became Birkbeck College, now a highly successful constituent part of London University, offering degree courses to part-time students.

The Great Exhibition of 1851 gave a fresh impetus to technical education, revealing the enormous industrial progress taking place in Europe. For the first but certainly not the last time foreign competition provided a stimulus for training initiatives in this country. In 1856 the Royal Society of Arts started a system of examinations for artisans, and four years later a Department of Science and Art was formed to establish a scheme of examinations in science and industrial design. A number of Mechanics Institutes developed into regional examination bodies, one of the best known being the Union of Lancashire and Cheshire Institutes. In 1869 the Livery Companies of the City of London began to finance initiatives to raise the standard of technical education and in 1878 the City and Guilds of London Institute was founded in order 'to provide a national system of technical education' (Lang, 1978).

Meanwhile, many of the Mechanics Institutes were developing into larger colleges. New colleges were being opened, including two founded by the City and Guilds of London Institute: Finsbury Technical College, which opened in 1883, and the Central Institution, in 1884. Evening institutes were also established and, following the 1902 Education Act, a number of junior technical schools opened for boys leaving school at 12 or 13 and preparing for an apprenticeship three years later. These schools, which sometimes had their own premises and sometimes shared with technical colleges, trained boys for local industry in small well-defined areas. Once apprenticed, many of the boys returned in the evenings for further instruction.

Night school, whether actually in school or in evening institutes or technical colleges, became the route to promotion, particularly after 1921 with the introduction of a national certificate system. The Ordinary and Higher National Certificates, entailing respectively three and two years' further study, included both theory and practical training and became the accepted route to professional engineering status. Night school continued to be the main way in which young men obtained a technical education throughout the first half of this century. By comparison, day-time study opportunities were few. In 1938, for example, there were only 20,000 full-time and 42,000 part-time day-release students receiving technical education.

THE LAST FIFTY YEARS

A major shift of emphasis was introduced by the 1944 Education Act, which imposed a statutory duty on LEAs 'to secure the provision for their area of adequate facilities for further education, that is to say, full-time and part-time education for persons over compulsory school age' (Education Act, 1944). There followed a massive expansion in further education that replaced the traditional evening classes with a range of full-time courses and day- and block-release opportunities that have continued for fifty years to extend and diversify with bewildering rapidity. By 1990 there were 582,000 full-time and 788,000 part-time students engaged in day-time further education. A total of 311,000 full-time and one-third of the part-time students were in the 16–19 age group. At the same time the colleges engaged in this work have developed a whole new range of evening courses, including many leisure activities and general interest options.

Further expansion is planned. In 1991 the government announced measures to encourage more school leavers to continue with their education or take up training places. In particular, further education is to be made more attractive and accessible by the availability of training credits – vouchers offered to those leaving full-time education at 16 or 17 which they can exchange for a course of vocational training. This scheme is to be phased in over five years with the intention that by 1996 all who leave full-time education at 16 or 17 will have the offer of a training credit.

Developments in further education over the last half-century have been on a scale totally different from that of the previous 150 years and the modern version of the technical college has a far wider curriculum than its earlier counterparts. Nevertheless, the traditions of technical education remain relevant to the role of colleges today. Like their various predecessors, the current providers of further education are, first and foremost, centres of vocational training. Their work reflects developments in the national economy and subsequent changes in the needs of local employers. Thus the decline in manufacturing, and particularly in heavy industry such as steel production and coal-mining, has resulted in a virtual collapse of the traditional apprentice system and of the courses associated with it. On the other hand, the greatly increased demand for trained personnel in business and office skills and in the leisure and service industries has created significant growth areas of work.

More specifically, further education has had to respond to successive government initiatives to improve the quality of the country's workforce through more effective and relevant training and retraining programmes. The last fifteen years have been a particularly active period in this respect. The belief that without incentives employers will pay insufficient attention to the country's crucial long-term training needs has led to a major increase in government expenditure on youth training.

This development has much to do with the problem of high unemployment and the need to find alternatives for school leavers not continuing with their education but unable to find a job. A series of youth training programmes designed to coordinate arrangements for unemployed school leavers began with the Youth Opportunities Programme (YOP) in 1977. This became the Youth Training Scheme (YTS) in 1983 which in turn gave way to Youth Training (YT) in 1990.

The current system is administered by 82 Training and Enterprise Councils (TECs), independent companies set up throughout England and Wales with multi-million-pound contracts from the government to encourage a variety of training and retraining initiatives. Boards of directors have been drawn from the senior management of local firms and public services. The TECs negotiate programmes of Youth Training and agree funding with numerous training suppliers, who may be well-established training organisations or companies formed specifically in response to the YT initiative. Some colleges have formed their own training supply companies, others are involved in providing off-the-job components of training purchased by other training organisations. Youth trainees prepare for National Vocational Qualifications (NVQs) at level 2 or beyond, or, where no NVQ yet exists, for equivalent qualifications. The government intends that ultimately all young people aged 16 and 17 will be given the opportunity of youth training if they want it.

THE FURTHER EDUCATION COLLEGE

Most technical colleges have now changed their name to *further education colleges* to reflect the breadth and diversity of their education and training programmes in the modern business world. Others, however, retain the designation *technical college* in recognition of their continuing training role in relation to the manufacturing industry. Also the term *technical* has a new relevance with regard to the rapid growth of high-tech businesses. Larger colleges are designated *colleges of technology* or, to emphasise the broad base of their work, *colleges of arts and technology*. There are also specialist institutions such as colleges of art, design or agriculture that offer courses within a restricted vocational range. These variations combine with a complex range of courses and levels of study to make further education a confusing world, not only to the layman but to many educationists and employers.

The term *FE college* is applied particularly to those 16+ colleges, 239 in number, offering courses at levels equivalent to those of the sixth form, but with the emphasis on a wide range of vocational subjects, training programmes and leisure activities. Many of these colleges, however, also offer courses leading to qualifications above GCE A level or its vocational equivalents. This work, traditionally designated *advanced further education* (AFE), overlaps with the provision in some higher education institutions.

This overlap is further complicated by the fact that many of the newer HE institutions, the polytechnics and colleges of higher education, also run *further education* courses. Until 1987 polytechnics and colleges of higher education came under the control of LEAs and combined their national or higher education function with a local or regional role within the strategic planning of an LEA. Many have retained a substantial amount of further education work, and a significant number of 16–19 students, from this earlier situation.

Another dimension has been given to further education college provision by the development of academic courses alongside the central vocational curriculum. GCE courses at both advanced and ordinary level were introduced for part-time students in the early post-war years. Then during the 1950s the colleges began to admit school leavers to full-time GCE courses. Some of these were grammar school pupils who had failed to meet the entry requirements of the sixth form. Others came from secondary modern schools, aspiring to qualifications that were not available in their schools.

This trend gathered pace in the 1960s and some colleges developed an extensive range of GCE subjects, including A level options and subject combinations that were not always available in the sixth form. One-year A levels were sometimes offered alongside or instead of the normal two-year courses. These alternatives to the traditional sixth form provision, combined with the adult atmosphere of the further education college, encouraged some potential sixth formers to transfer from maintained and independent schools to colleges for their A level work.

THE TERTIARY COLLEGE

In areas where further education institutions had successfully developed dual academic and vocational provision, the FE college suggested itself as an alternative to the sixth form college to LEAs interested in a form of secondary reorganisation involving a break at 16+. As early as 1959 the Crowther Report had floated the idea of a 16–19 college that combined the sixth form and technical college curricula for full-time students. Ten years later, Sir William Alexander, Chairman of the Association of Education Committees, advocated that 'the secondary stage of education should be limited to the age of 16 . . . and that there should be established tertiary colleges providing both full- and part-time education from this stage to 18+' (Alexander, 1969:19).

The first tertiary college was formed in 1970 when sixth formers in Exeter were transferred from the schools to the city's further education college. This was followed by similar reorganisation schemes in Barnstaple (Devon) and Nelson and Colne (Lancashire) in 1972 and in Bridgwater and Street (Somerset) in 1973. By 1992 there were 57 tertiary colleges accommodating 90,000 full-time students aged 16–19. The colleges range in size from 500 to 2,700 full-time students, on average twice the size of a sixth form college. As with all further education colleges, they also have a large number of part-time, day-release and evening students. Some of the largest colleges, those with over 2,000 full-time students, have more than 10,000 part-timers. Colleges of this size are thus operating on a scale quite different from that of even the largest sixth form college or secondary school.

The original tertiary college concept was to bring all 16+ courses in a specific geographical area together in one institution, instead of presenting them as competing alternatives in separate establishments. Thus the tertiary college was seen as the ultimate in a cost-effective, fully comprehensive system of 16+ provision. However, in some urban areas tertiary colleges have been developed alongside school sixth forms and/or sixth form colleges, creating a more complex system of 16–19 provision. In Swindon, pupils leaving school have a choice of two colleges, one a traditional further education establishment, the other run under FE regulations but following the Crowther Report recommendation in admitting only full-time students aged 16–19.

The normal method of forming a tertiary college has been

simply to transfer school sixth form provision to an existing further education college. There have, however, been a number of variations on this strategy. In Andover (Hampshire), for example, a purpose-built tertiary college was opened in 1974 to replace the existing grammar school sixth form and to provide vocational courses for a town that previously had no FE college. In some other areas where there had previously been no FE provision sixth form colleges were re-designated tertiary colleges, adding FE work to their academic courses and consequently then coming under FE regulations. Examples are Skelmersdale in Lancashire and Brockenhurst in Hampshire.

In recent years a number of tertiary colleges have been formed by the merging of further education and sixth form colleges, examples being in Henley (Oxfordshire) and Harrow (Middlesex). Several urban areas are served by more than one tertiary college. Sheffield initially established seven but has subsequently given notice of a likely trend in the future by merging these into one huge college with the equivalent of 11,000 full-time students.

The considerable variations of size and role that exist within the category *tertiary* produce colleges of very different character. However, they have significant features in common and the combination of further education and sixth form work produces a situation that distinguishes the tertiary college from a traditional FE institution. In particular, the average age of the students is lower and the needs of the 16–19 age group of paramount importance. This has significant organisational and managerial implications, not least for the colleges, care systems.

INDEPENDENT FURTHER EDUCATION

There is nothing to prevent anyone in Britain from selling education or training to those above the statutory school-leaving age. The only constraints are the normal legal requirements applicable to all private businesses: there are no minimal standards of quality or efficiency that have to be met, not even a registration requirement. Not surprisingly, there exists a plethora of institutions offering a diverse range of further education courses in competition with the maintained sector.

A major area of direct competition is in academic work. Many independent FE institutions concentrate on GCE and GCSE courses, with a sharp focus on examination preparation and success. These are the tutorial colleges, or 'crammers', which offer intensive training in examination technique and cater particularly for those requiring short revision or re-take courses.

There are also a number of independent FE colleges offering a broader educational experience whilst still providing intensive tuition in examination courses. These institutions offer fee-paying students an alternative to the sixth forms of an independent school and their prospectuses stress the advantages of a college-style education over that of a school. They are very popular with students from abroad who seek to enhance their chances of admission to a British university by taking A levels in this country. A third of the places in academic independent FE colleges are taken up by foreign students. The source varies from year to year with fluctuating currency restrictions in different countries, but Malaysia, Hong Kong and Singapore are major contributors. An increasing number of students are coming from EC countries, whilst African sources are in decline.

Another significant category of independent FE comprises the business and secretarial colleges. These offer a wide range of nationally recognised vocational qualifications and sometimes additional diplomas and certificates of their own. A large part of independent FE is concerned with the provision of specialist vocational courses. Some of this work is in direct competition with the maintained sector, for example in areas such as childcare, hairdressing, beauty therapy and catering.

The independent sector has established certain areas of the curriculum where it is the main provider. Prominent in this category are the language schools, particularly those that specialise in teaching English for specific purposes. There has been a rapid growth in recent years in courses in English as a foreign language (EFL) and English as a second language (ESL). There are also many institutions that specialise in the arts and the media, particularly dance. A wide range of creative arts and crafts establishments provide leisure and interest courses as well as vocational training.

Another category of independent FE establishment offers alternative approaches to the vocational training available in the maintained sector, for example specific forms of horticulture or animal welfare, specialist catering such as cordon bleu cooking, alternative approaches to agriculture, such as organic farming, or to health care and child welfare, such as the Montessori method of educating very young children.

Independent FE institutions are virtually impossible to classify. They range from very small establishments catering for a mere handful of students to one establishment with an enrolment of 12,000. The courses are constantly changing in response to market forces and the smaller institutions are subject to the same fluctuating fortunes and insecurity as other small businesses. There are single sex and coeducational establishments, those catering specifically for full-time or part-time students and others that combine the two. Courses run from periods of a few days to two years. The certificates and diplomas awarded may be the same nationally accepted qualifications as those available in the maintained sector or may be designed by professional bodies or the institutions themselves. The latter may be highly regarded and widely recognised or have very little currency; they may indicate a high level of achievement or be little more than attendance/participation certificates.

At one time the DES monitored the quality and efficiency of independent FE establishments, but this practice was discontinued in 1982, partly because the cost was considered too great but also because it was thought that the private sector should be self-regulating. In response to the void created by this decision the British Accreditation Council for Independent Further and Higher Education was formed in 1984. The BAC is a limited company, recognised as a registered charity, which provides objective assessment of premises, resources, teaching standards, student welfare arrangements and the legal and financial viability of institutions. Once accredited, institutions have to submit an annual report on developments and agree to be reinspected every five years. The BAC has accredited 75 institutions. Forty per cent of these are GCE and GCSE tutorial colleges; the others offer professional and vocational qualifications leading to many different careers.

The BAC works closely with two other accrediting bodies, the Council for the Accreditation of Correspondence Colleges, which has been in existence since 1969, and the British Council, which took over responsibility for accrediting English-language schools, the largest single group of specialist independent colleges, when the government discontinued its monitoring role in 1982. These three bodies publish a joint directory of accredited independent colleges, a total of 343 institutions.

Participation in all these accreditation schemes is entirely voluntary and many institutions are unaffected by them. The quality of provision in the independent FE sector is therefore as variable as in any other area of private business. Since independent FE establishments are not required to register, there is no means even of determining how many there are. However, the BAC estimates that there must be in the region of 1,500 institutions with a total enrolment of one million students.

Chapter 3

The academic curriculum

SPECIALISATION

The transition from compulsory schooling to 16–19 education is marked by an abrupt change of curriculum. Until the age of 16 all pupils follow a programme of study aimed at providing a broad general education. Post-GCSE courses are much more narrowly focused, being designed as a preparation and means of qualifying for a specific higher education course or career: they are a progression route. There are in fact two distinct routes: the academic and the vocational.

The 16–19 academic curriculum is made up of a number of discrete subject specialisms. In that respect it resembles its 14–16 counterpart, but the approach is entirely different. The GCSE curriculum consists of a range of basic subjects, the majority of which all pupils study. The A level curriculum comprises a much greater range of specialisms from which students are normally expected to choose only three. Whereas pre-16 the aim is breadth and variety of experience, post-16 the emphasis is on specialisation and in-depth study of a limited field of enquiry. To this end, the three courses followed are often drawn from the same subject area.

The suddenness of this transition from the general to the specific is a source of much surprise, even amazement, to educationists from most other western countries, where general education normally gives way to specialisation much more gradually and at a later stage. For example, in American high schools students are positively discouraged from specialisation and even at university they follow a broadly-based programme that includes English for scientists and science courses for those taking arts subjects. The system is a modular one that requires students to gain credits in several different subject areas. A combination of compulsory modules and electives enables a gradual move towards specialisation for those who require it whilst maintaining a broad and balanced programme of study. The French *Baccalauréat* lasts for three years and is a multi-subject examination. Typically, candidates take written and oral examinations in seven core and specialist subjects. The German *Abitur*, usually taken at the age of 19, consists of seven or eight subjects, including a modern foreign language, mathematics or natural science, and German.

SYLLABUS PROVISION: THE GCE EXAMINATION BOARDS

The English A level curriculum is made up of syllabuses designed by eight GCE examination boards, all private businesses linked with particular universities or groups of universities. Between them these boards offer and examine nearly 400 syllabuses in more than 70 subjects, a range that reflects the diversity of the higher education courses for which they are primarily a preparation. The majority of A level subjects are in fact minority interests, the demand for which justifies only one board offering a syllabus.

The bulk of the GCE examination boards' work relates to a group of twelve subjects that account for 80 per cent of the A level candidature. In most of these subjects all the boards offer at least one syllabus and sometimes more than one. There is considerable overlap in the different syllabuses offered in these popular subjects, the boards having entered into an agreement with the universities in 1983 that 'in major curricular areas' there should be a common core of content which would form a substantial part of all A level syllabuses bearing the same subject title.

There have been several attempts to rationalise A level syllabus provision and to reduce the number of syllabuses available in each subject. The School Examinations and Assessment Council (SEAC), established by the 1988 Education Reform Act, has had this exercise as one of its briefs. The boards, however, are resistant to such initiatives as their livelihood depends upon their maintaining a share of the candidature in popular A level subjects. Also, rationalisation implies an eventual reduction in the number of boards. The boards argue that, although there is inevitably a degree of duplication in syllabuses with the same subject title, there are significant differences of emphasis that reflect the individual boards' responsiveness to the needs of their particular centres.

There are indeed considerable differences in the clientele of the various boards; the Associated Examining Board (AEB), for example, has a very high number of FE colleges, whereas the Oxford and Cambridge Board caters primarily for the public schools. These differences are being countered to some extent by an increasing tendency for institutions to become centres for several boards and to allow their subject departments to choose whichever board's syllabus is most in tune with their own curricular thinking and method of course delivery.

SYLLABUS PROVISION: THE RANGE OFFERED BY SCHOOLS AND COLLEGES

Students' choice of A level programme depends, in the first instance, on the range of options offered by their school or college. The normal provision is 12–20 subjects, but this is considerably extended in the larger institutions.

The most popular courses are those in English, mathematics, the three sciences, history, geography, economics, sociology, French and art; the majority of students choose their programme from these subjects. Common additions to this popular core of subjects are music, German, design/technology, religious studies, government/politics, computer science and geology.

There are interesting variations in the provision made by different kinds of institution. FE colleges often add a number of what might be termed 'vocational' A levels to the basic range - subjects such as law, accounting and theatre studies. Psychology and communication studies are also popular FE options. These subjects have yet to acquire respectability in most public and grammar schools, which also omit sociology, one of the most popular subjects nationally.

A feature of the curriculum in these schools is the wide range of languages on offer, often as many as five or six. French, German and Latin are standard, with Spanish, Russian and Classical Greek popular additions. Other minority languages are occasionally offered or provided in response to demand - Italian and even Arabic and Japanese. Ancient History or Classical Civilisation is a frequent addition, bringing the range of subjects available in public and grammar schools to about 20.

Some large colleges offer 40-50 options, including alternative syllabuses in popular subjects - human and/or social biology in addition to the traditional syllabus; economic and/or social history as well as British and European; different media in art; English language as an alternative to the normal literature course; special syllabuses in the physical sciences, geography and mathematics. This curricular variety may be supported by departmental teams that contain specialists teaching different aspects of a subject in a similar way to the universities and other HE institutions.

This is one of the clear advantages of size. With a range of staff expertise available and the timetabling flexibility afforded by large numbers and extensive accommodation, large colleges can maintain a wide range of options. Moreover, they are well placed to respond quickly and flexibly to new initiatives and alternative approaches. For example, if a new syllabus becomes available, such as the London Board's geography 16-19 or the Cambridge history project, this can be introduced alongside existing syllabuses and students given a choice. Over a period of time the new approach can be evaluated and compared with established syllabuses. A decision can then be taken either to offer the preferred option or to continue providing alternatives.

This flexibility is not open to smaller 16-19 units. Indeed small sixth forms have difficulty in providing even the basic subjects. Alternative syllabuses, except perhaps in mathematics, are luxuries that can rarely be considered. In any sixth form with fewer than 100 students viable groups are likely in only about half a dozen subjects and maintaining an adequate choice of options in this situation entails some difficult management decisions.

In the past there has often been an assumption that small sixth form groups have to be paid for by larger classes lower down the school. For those who find this strategy unacceptable the alternatives are: reducing the time allocation for undersubscribed A level courses, combining small year 12 and 13 classes, and allowing A level students to join other age groups in independent learning situations that free staff to work with individuals or small groups in turn. Community schools have increased the size of groups by enrolling adults in daytime classes. They have also had the option to broaden the curriculum by giving their students access to adult evening classes. Some non-community schools have similarly extended the range of subjects they offer through arrangements with nearby FE colleges.

STUDENTS' PROGRAMMES OF STUDY

The size of institution affects not only the range of subjects that can be offered but also the extent to which the various combinations of subject that students wish to study can be timetabled. Constraints on student choice of subject combination are not, however, merely a matter of timetabling expediency. The specialist tradition has militated against free choice, the assumption having always been that students should normally study a group of closely associated subjects that form a recognised career or higher education route. Examples are a science or languages grouping or English and history plus a language or other arts subject. Whilst such programmes do not limit students to a specific 18+ course or vocation they do indicate a direction and, to varying degrees, narrow a student's HE and career choices. This applies particularly to HE courses and careers in science, entry to which may well be dependent upon a specific set of A level qualifications.

The tradition of choosing between a science or arts group of subjects has been so strong that for many years the science/arts distinction was marked by separately designated, and sometimes physically divided, science and arts sixth forms. This division still exists in some public and grammar schools but has lost much of its old rigidity with the acceptance of an increasing number of subjects deemed to belong to both divisions. Geography has long been seen as a logical part of either a science or arts combination and of course can lead in HE to either a BSc or BA degree. Economics and mathematics are likewise ambivalent and, as A level foreign languages have lost their total preoccupation with literature and become more concerned with everyday communication skills, their relevance to scientists as well as arts students has been acknowledged. Some public and grammar schools no longer recognise science/arts divisions.

Colleges and comprehensive schools have had no tradition of classifying students as 'science' or 'arts'. Their aim is usually to allow for as many subject combinations as possible. Where staffing and timetable constraints result in a limited choice, however, the traditional groupings often receive priority. In the bigger colleges which offer a free, or virtually free, choice of subject combination there is a growing tendency for students to study those subjects in which they are most interested and have been most successful – regardless of whether they represent a recognised career path. Higher education's increasingly diverse provision and more flexible admissions criteria have encouraged this process.

Modular approaches to syllabus design offer even greater flexibility in constructing A level programmes. The Wessex and Cambridge schemes, for example, break A level courses down into a number of self-contained, separately assessed units and give students an element of choice within a subject. SEAC, constrained by the government's insistence on the traditional specialist approach, has opposed programmes made up of modules from different subject areas. Such flexibility, however, is normal in other countries and not uncommon in this country in higher education.

There remains, however, a crucial tension in the 16–19 academic curriculum between the natural desire of many students to follow a varied programme of study and the need to recognise that there remain many career and HE routes, particularly in the sciences, that still require students to follow a narrowly-focused combination of A levels. The traditional norm of three subjects provides no room for manoeuvre: if a group of allied subjects is needed for a specific career then variety has to be sacrificed.

ATTEMPTS TO BROADEN THE A LEVEL CURRICULUM

The disadvantages of premature specialisation have been well-documented and frequent attempts made to broaden the 16–19 academic curriculum. In 1960 A. D. C. Peterson, Director of the Oxford Institute of Education, argued the case for reform in an influential publication *Arts and Science Sides in the Sixth Form*. Following the publication of this pamphlet, three major conferences were held in Oxford for heads of independent and maintained schools at which Peterson advocated reducing the content of A level syllabuses by a third to allow for a four-subject curriculum in which all students would cross the science/arts divide, scientists taking one arts subject, arts students studying one science. The heads were impressed, but daunted by the prospect of reforming the A level system. Instead they turned their attention to the softer option of improving their provision for non-examined general studies. Perhaps C. P. Snow's warning of the difficulties of broadening the academic curriculum was fresh in many minds from his previous year's Rede Lecture:

Nearly everyone will agree that our school education is too specialised. But nearly everyone feels that it is outside the wit of man to alter it.

(Snow, 1959)

The International Baccalaureate

Peterson went on to play a major part in the establishment of the International Baccalaureate (IB), a qualification based on a unified course of study in six subjects drawn from several different disciplines. In the IB all students study maths, a science, social studies, two languages and a course in world literature in translation. A fine-arts subject can also be taken as an alternative to a further study from one of the compulsory disciplines.

The first pilot group of students sat the IB examination in 1969 and the qualification quickly became accepted by the universities. The IB was intended to meet the special needs of international and multi-national schools throughout the world. In recent years, however, many other institutions in this country have given serious consideration to the IB as an alternative to A levels. In 1993 23 UK centres will be entering candidates for the IB examinations; they include some of the larger public schools and a number of FE and sixth form colleges.

Two-tier attempts to reform the A level curriculum

There have been repeated calls to change the over-specialised A level system in the three decades since Peterson's abortive attempt at reform. Numerous research projects, consultative exercises and national debates have addressed the need to broaden the 16–19 academic curriculum. Formal recommendations emerged at regular intervals – the Q and F proposals in 1969, N and F in 1974 and Intermediate Levels in 1979. All proposed a two-tier examination system that would keep A levels more or less intact but extend the range of students' programmes of study.

None of these initiatives gained favour. The reformers pointed out that in a two-tier system teachers and students would inevitably attach less importance to the lower-level courses, thereby undermining the concept of breadth. Traditionalists were concerned that even these modest attempts to broaden students' studies would dilute the A level experience so that students would be less well prepared for their higher education specialism.

AS levels

In 1987 the government reintroduced an idea from pre-A level days – the subsidiary subjects of the old Higher School Certificate. A range of Advanced Supplementaries was added to the A level curriculum. AS levels are two-year examination courses designed to make the same academic demands as A level, but containing half the content and, theoretically, receiving half the time allocation. Students can take an AS in addition to their three A levels or two or three AS levels in place of one A level.

Despite heavy government backing and publicity, AS levels have been slow to gain acceptance and many small sixth forms have simply not had the resources or timetabling flexibility to offer them. Little interest has been shown in the two A level and two/three AS level option, but 5 per cent of university applicants in 1990 had taken one AS level in addition to three A levels.

The broadening function of AS levels has been a conspicuous failure. The expressed aim of the Advanced Supplementaries was for students to choose the new examination courses from subject areas other than those from which their A level courses were taken. There was, however, no prescription to this effect and the new courses have tended to reinforce rather than counteract the specialist approach. A survey in 1990 showed that for every student who was using an AS course to provide a contrast to an A level programme, three were doing so to complement it. Some schools and colleges have used AS courses simply as a one-year stepping stone to A level in the same subject, or made dual A and AS entries to cover weaker candidates against A level failure.

Successive governments in the last 30 years have failed to

respond to the well-demonstrated need for reform of the 16–19 system. For the last 12 years, preservation of 'the gold standard' of A level has been a cornerstone of education policy. In introducing Additional Supplementaries, during Mrs Thatcher's third term of office, the government sought to appease the growing lobby for reform whilst reaffirming its own faith in A levels.

When AS levels were introduced in 1987 a committee was set up under the chairmanship of Gordon Higginson, Vice-Chancellor of Southampton University, with the following terms of reference:

> In the light of the Government's commitment to retain General Certificate of Education (GCE) Advanced Level Examinations as an essential means for setting standards of excellence, and with the aim of maintaining or improving the present character and rigorous standards of these examinations:
>
> To recommend the principles that should govern GCE A level syllabuses and their assessment, so that consistency in the essential content and the assessment of subjects is secured.
>
> To set out a plan of action for the subsequent detailed professional work required to give effect to these recommendations.
>
> (DES, 1988b)

The Higginson Committee's proposals, 1988

As soon as it began its work, the Higginson Committee became keenly aware of the widespread dissatisfaction with the system it was set up to endorse. The Committee reported that 'on nearly all the major issues a remarkable consensus emerged from the evidence' that it received. In particular, there was constant reiteration of the need for the 16–19 academic curriculum 'to provide a broad and valuable experience' in its own right and not to be seen primarily as a preparation for the next stage. Well aware that it was stepping outside its narrowly-focused brief, the Committee rejected the *raison d'être* for the specialised approach of the A level system – to groom a selected minority for Higher Education:

> The most fundamental error in the traditional GCE/A level system was that each stage was designed to be suited for those

who were going on to the next. Schoolchildren who were not good enough to go on were regarded as expendable. The other view, which seems to be held in every other advanced country, is that each stage of education should be designed for the main body of those who take it and the following stage has to start from where the previous stage ended.

(DES, 1988b)

The Higginson Committee gave articulate expression to the consensus for greater breadth in the 16–19 academic curriculum, both in terms of the number of subjects studied and the nature of the experience within them. The Committee's major recommendation was that the normal A level programme should consist of five subjects instead of three. The aim was to design 'leaner, tougher syllabuses' with a reduced content and a sharper focus on conceptual understanding. There was no prescription for a science/arts mix, but the fact that students would follow five subjects would greatly increase the likelihood of a broadly-based programme of study.

The 'Higginson proposals', as they became known, were dismissed by the then Secretary of State, Kenneth Baker, before anyone had a chance to read them. Immediately the newly-formed School Examinations and Assessment Council was asked to take due note of the government's reaffirmation of faith in the existing A level system and to undertake measures to promote AS levels as a means of providing greater breadth. Meanwhile, the Higginson proposals were welcomed by the Opposition and became part of official Labour party education policy in the years preceding the 1992 general election.

The School Examinations and Assessment Council's proposals, 1990

In pursuing its brief, SEAC sought to reconcile the increasingly divergent views of the government and those of the great majority of educationists as represented by the Higginson Committee's report. The Council's solution put forward in 1990, after yet another lengthy consultation exercise, was an ingenious inversion of the relationship between A and AS levels. An extended range of AS courses would 'embody the essential skills, knowledge and learning which constitute the A level standard' and become the basic units from which students would build their programme of academic studies. A levels, probably reduced in number, would provide additional contexts in which students who were so inclined would be able to extend and illustrate their grasp of a discipline. 'This arrangement of AS and A examination courses would enable students more readily to assemble a broad study programme since the unit of study would be one sixth of the normal full-time programme rather than one third' (SEAC, 1990a).

It was envisaged that all students would be likely to take at least two AS courses and the opportunity would exist for them to choose up to six. The implication was that four subjects (two AS and two A level) would become the norm for prospective university applicants, but students might well extend their range of subjects to five or six.

The government was again faced with a challenge to the traditional A level system. This time ministers, well aware of the direction in which the Council was moving, voiced their opposition to reform before the proposals were made public. SEAC, however, had to wait five months for a formal reply to its recommendations. It eventually came in the form of the 1991 White Paper *Education and Training for the 21st Century*, which stressed yet again the government's strong commitment to the retention of A levels in their traditional form.

VARIATIONS IN STUDENTS' PROGRAMMES OF STUDY

Whilst the standard academic programme for post-16 students remains three A levels, few institutions can claim this as an absolute norm. In the public and grammar schools, and in many sixth form and tertiary colleges, large numbers of able students study four A levels, usually by adding a second mathematics course to a mathematics and science subject combination. In comprehensive schools and all types of 16+ college there is provision for students to follow one or two A levels in combination with other courses.

The extension of the comprehensive principle to post-16 education has led to the development of an extensive alternative academic curriculum for those who need to improve their basic qualifications. Since the introduction in 1986 of the General Certificate of Secondary Education (GCSE) many one-year courses have been designed specifically for older students. Of the same standard as their 16+ counterparts, these 'mature' syllabuses include an extensive range of more specialist subjects than the normal 14–16 courses. Some of the larger colleges offer as many as 40 GCSE alternatives: in addition to syllabuses in the basic school subjects there are options such as law, politics, psychology, media studies, photography, surveying, accounts, electronics, information and control technology.

These one-year courses can usually be taken in conjunction with A level work, for example by those studying one or two A levels. However, large numbers of students enter the colleges and comprehensive school sixth forms for a one-year academic programme consisting of several (most typically four) GCSE courses. These students will be seeking to enter employment or to start either A level or vocational courses at 17.

The continued demand for post-16 one-year academic courses has led to proposals for a one-year intermediate examination specifically designed for those who wish to gain further academic rather than vocational qualifications, but for whom A level is too difficult. Dr Anderson, Head Master of Eton College, has led a public school lobby for this strategy, which is seen as a means of enabling more young people to continue with academic work without lowering the standard of entry to A level courses. The Intermediate courses would have a dual function by replacing AS levels as a means of broadening A level students' programmes of study. An interesting suggestion is that they could also fulfil a similar role for vocational students by providing them with an opportunity to continue with some academic studies alongside their vocational training.

The trends in 16–19 education are towards much more open access and greater flexibility in the design of students' programmes of study. The old barriers between academic disciplines are at last being broken down. Increasingly, too, students have opportunities to combine courses at different levels of the academic curriculum, instead of having to mark time in one subject area because of inadequate qualifications in another. A natural extension of such flexibility is the move to encourage students to combine academic and vocational components in their programmes of study. This significant development is discussed in the next chapter.

Chapter 4

The vocational curriculum

THE SYSTEM OF QUALIFICATIONS

The *raison d'être* for vocational qualifications is the need for different professions and occupations to establish standards of competence for those employed in them. There are some 370 professional bodies and industrial and trade organisations that set vocational standards and most of these are involved in some aspect of training, examining and/or accrediting.

In addition, there are several major independent awarding bodies that provide national certification across a wide spectrum of professions and occupations. These include the RSA Examinations Board, now a separate organisation from the Royal Society of Arts, and the City and Guilds of London Institute, one of the nineteenth-century pioneers of vocational education. The RSA Examinations Board concentrates mainly on business/commercial qualifications leading to all office-based occupations; in addition, it offers certification for those seeking employment in the distributive trades and various aspects of road transport. The City and Guilds examination courses are a preparation for employment in many branches of light and heavy industry, including agriculture, horticulture and service industries such as catering and tourism.

Further extensive provision in business and technological fields is offered by the Business and Technician Education Council (BTEC), a self-financing validating body appointed by the government in 1983. BTEC brought together the Technician Education and the Business Education Councils, related executive bodies that had been set up in 1973 and 1974 respectively, following the publication of the Haslegrave Report

on technician education and examinations. Other major awarding bodies are the Pitman Examinations Institute (PEI) and the
London Chamber of Commerce (LCC).

These examining and certificating bodies are all highly entrepreneurial and, although earlier gentlemen's agreements
established different vocation territories, there is increasing
overlap and competition for the student market. This, together
with the large number of other organisations offering vocational
certification, has led to an enormous range of qualifications.
There is considerable duplication in some of the major occupations, which leads to confusion among employers and students
concerning the relative value of qualifications and the way in
which they relate to each other. At the same time, the haphazard
way in which the system has developed has resulted in other
occupations being without an appropriate set of properly graded
qualifications. Discriminatory rules and age limits have often
restricted access to vocational qualifications and concern has
been expressed that a considerably lower proportion of the UK
workforce holds relevant qualifications than in other major
industrial countries.

NATIONAL VOCATIONAL QUALIFICATIONS

In 1986 a Review of Vocational Qualifications (RVQ) was
undertaken which led to the formation of a National Council for
Vocational Qualifications (NCVQ) with a brief to improve the
quality of vocational training, to widen access to qualifications
and to raise the standard of the British workforce. The NCVQ has
liaised with employers, trade unions and professional organisations to establish standards of competence for each area of
employment and worked with approved awarding bodies to
translate these standards into a set of nationally recognised
qualifications.

The NCVQ has constructed a framework of National
Vocational Qualifications (NVQs) covering all major occupations and providing a common format for measuring quality and
good practice. It shows clearly the progression routes that one
can follow from lower to higher levels and from one set of
qualifications to another related group. A database gives full
details of all qualifications and the separate units within them.

The units that go to make up an NVQ provide a measure of

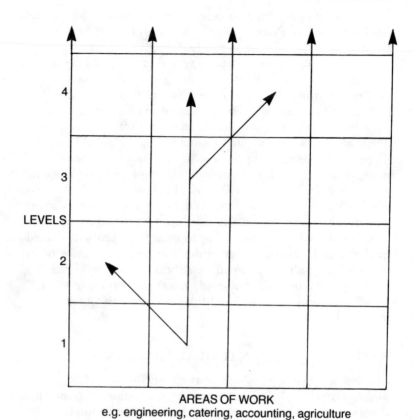

AREAS OF WORK
e.g. engineering, catering, accounting, agriculture

Figure 4.1   The National Vocational Qualifications framework
Source: NCVQ: A Brief Guide (NCVQ 1990)

student performance in different work roles against agreed national standards. Students and employees make their own choice of units and also decide how and where they work to achieve the required levels of competence. Assessment makes use of different forms of evidence of achievement. A separate NVQ credit is awarded for each unit and credits can be accumulated at the student's or employee's own pace. Successful completion of a set of units, varying in number from occupation to occupation, qualifies for the award of a specifically named NVQ by one of the recognised awarding bodies, such as BTEC, RSA, City and

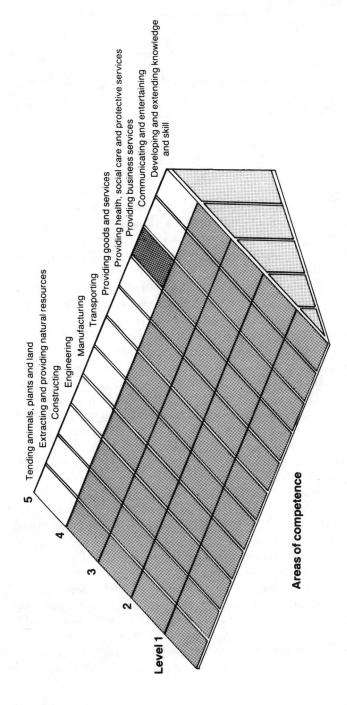

Figure 4.2 The NVQ framework: areas and levels of competence
Source: The NVQ Framework (NCVQ, 1992)

Guilds. Awarding bodies approved by the NCVQ are allowed to accredit qualifications as NVQs and assign them to one of the levels of the framework according to agreed criteria. There are five levels in the national framework and, by the end of 1992, level 1–4 qualifications were available to over 80 per cent of the British workforce. It is estimated that by 1995 one million NVQ awards will have been made.

VOCATIONAL PROGRAMMES OF STUDY

Vocational courses give practical experience and training at different levels in a range of work-related tasks, skills and competences relevant to a particular occupation or group of closely-related occupations. City and Guilds courses are presented to institutions as a complete course of study made up of a number of related units. Some RSA courses follow this pattern whilst others consist of single-subject syllabuses which institutions package into a coherent course.

BTEC courses consist of a combination of core and optional units from which colleges form an integrated programme to meet particular needs, incorporating units of their own design if they so wish. Major integrative assignments, which form part of the coursework assessment, draw on the work in different units.

The common factor in these variations is the fact that the units of a vocational course constitute a single package, a coherent integrated programme of study. This is a major difference between vocational and academic programmes. The components of an A level programme are not only discrete subject specialisms, but separate courses offered and taught by different departments and members of staff, often with their own distinctive policies and methods of course delivery. Although made up of a number of units, a vocational course is conceived as an entity and usually delivered by a group of staff working together as a course team.

Vocational courses are, by definition, much more closely related to particular occupations than academic programmes of study, but many of the skills and personal competences that they develop have a general application. Even highly job-specific courses entail background work and related studies; for example, the City and Guilds basic craft certificate course in hairdressing involves applied science, art and design, hygiene, communication skills and salon organisation, as well as all aspects of practical hairdressing, manicure, cosmetic make-up and wigmaking. At one time general education components of vocational studies were taught as quite separate entities, but they have become increasingly the responsibility of the course team and integrated into the rest of the course.

In response to the criticism that in the past vocational pro-grammes have been too narrowly job-specific, first-level courses, in particular, have sought to stress the general application of the skills they teach. The Certificate of Pre-Vocational Educa-tion (CPVE) was introduced to provide a one-year transition from school to work for 'students of a wide ability range with varied interests and aptitudes and with varying degrees of vocational commitment' (DES, 1984). The CPVE was a flexible framework for one-year pre-vocational programmes of study devised by institutions and often varying from student to student. However, from the outset those pioneering this new approach found it difficult to resist the inexorable drift back to a narrower vocational focus.

The CPVE's lack of clear progression routes posed particular problems for the NCVQ and in 1990 John MacGregor, the then Secretary of State, asked City and Guilds to take over responsibility for the new certificate from the joint body pre-viously running it and to make the examination more rigorous in terms of its outcomes. The 'pre-vocational' description has been dropped from the title and the certificate re-named the City and Guilds Diploma of Vocational Education. There are three levels – Foundation (pre-16), Intermediate (NVQ2) and National (NVQ3). The Intermediate level equates with the old CPVE but the requirements are more specific and include substantial work in a particular vocational area. The development and assessment of transferable skills and the inclusion of work experience are important features of the Diploma of Vocational Education at all levels.

The demise of the CPVE had much to do with the introduction by BTEC in 1986 of a First Diploma that sought a compromise between the pre-vocational approach and narrow job-specific training. The BTEC First Diploma identifies clear progression routes, but to broad career areas, such as business and finance, the caring professions, distribution and the leisure industry. The programmes are designed to develop transferable skills and to keep students' options reasonably open.

The government endorsed this approach in 1991 by asking the NCVQ to develop a number of General NVQs that would prepare students for employment in a range of related occupations, without requiring them to make a specific career decision. GNVQs are intended to offer a general preparation for employment and higher-level qualifications and to keep open the option of students' proceeding to higher education. They assess the skills, knowledge and understanding that underpin a range of NVQs within a broad occupational area. They thus build on the work done by BTEC, RSA, City and Guilds and other awarding bodies in the field of general vocational education. Working groups have drawn up GNVQ specifications at levels 2 and 3 in five broad occupational areas: leisure and tourism, manufacturing, health and care, business and administration, and art and design. A phased introduction of GNVQs, using over 90 centres, began in September 1992.

The nature of vocational courses is constantly changing in response to the demands of the workplace. The need for a broad range of transferable skills and personal competences reflects the flexibility and adaptability required in many of today's work situations. In addition, each department has to respond to more specific developments in the occupations for which it provides training. The need for technician rather than craft skills has significantly altered the work undertaken by engineering and building departments. Business studies departments frequently have to revise their approaches and to renew their equipment in response to significant developments in office practice and technology. All departments have experienced a shift from part-time day- and block-release work to full-time courses.

THE PROVIDERS OF VOCATIONAL EDUCATION

The vocational curriculum has traditionally been the preserve of further education colleges. Although an increasing number of schools and sixth form colleges are now offering vocational courses, they are usually limited to a few occupational areas and certainly not comparable to the extensive development of academic courses by FE colleges.

Maintained FE colleges normally offer a wide range of courses in key vocational areas. Engineering and building departments have adapted to rather less dominant roles than in the past, but survive in a different form in most establishments. Business studies departments have become major providers, preparing students for careers in accountancy, banking, insurance, administration and management, and offering a complex programme of courses at different levels for potential data entry operators, audio or word-processing secretaries, receptionists and personal assistants. The increased opportunities in the service industries are reflected in courses in retail and distribution; fashion, art and design; travel, hotel management, catering and leisure services; hairdressing and beauty therapy; health services and community care. In addition, institutions often develop their own specialities and, between them, the colleges offer training in almost every conceivable occupation, from toymaking to baking, mastic asphalting to embalming, book-keeping to bee-keeping.

The range of courses available in any one college will depend upon two main factors - size and location. The larger the college the more options are possible. A small college in a rural part of Suffolk or Norfolk may have an enrolment of 800–900 full- and part-time day students, whereas large urban colleges have many thousands of students. The curriculum is also partly determined by the needs of local industry and commerce and the job opportunities they offer. Thus, although certain qualifications required by major industries and business occupations will be found in nearly all non-specialist colleges, the FE curriculum in a northern town that retains its heavy industry will obviously have a different emphasis to that of a college serving a west country holiday resort or a high-tech area in the south.

The national drive to increase participation rates in full-time further education has encouraged FE colleges to diversify and extend their curricular provision. Similar encouragement is being given to the schools sector: in 1990 the government agreed to allow BTEC to offer its First Diploma courses in institutions run under schools regulations and, in the following year, the 1991 government White Paper called upon schools and sixth form colleges to extend their vocational work and admit part-time and adult students to post-16 courses.

The concentration of academic work in one set of institutions and practical/vocational work in another has persisted longer at 16+ than 11+, but there has been a steady erosion of the idea that schools and sixth form colleges should concern themselves with one type of course and FE institutions with another. The tertiary college was seen as the institution that would break down these barriers completely, bringing the full range of both academic and vocational courses together under one roof and ultimately enabling students to transfer freely between the two, even to follow a mixed programme.

Colleges have worked hard at turning the tertiary ideal into reality, encouraging mixed economy programmes and even putting together their own packages of GCE/GCSE and vocational work for specific groups of students. For example, as an alternative to the BTEC National Diploma in Media Studies the Accrington and Rossendale College in Lancashire offers a Media Studies with A levels course which prepares students for qualification in three A levels, the City and Guilds Diploma in Journalism or Video Production and the College's own Diploma in Media Studies.

A City and Guilds pilot scheme launched in 1991 offers a national framework and qualification for broadly-based studies. The Technological Baccalaureate requires students to follow, alongside their other courses, a core curriculum that develops transferable skills in a technological and commercial context. Success in the core curriculum alone results in a pass. A credit is awarded to students who successfully combine the core curriculum with an NVQ level 3. Students passing three A levels and the core curriculum obtain a distinction.

Such schemes make heavy demands on students, as the means of broadening programmes of study is to add another dimension to the normal course. This demonstrates the practical difficulty of combining academic and vocational courses. Most vocational courses are complete programmes entailing a full-time commitment. Not only does this militate against vocational students simultaneously studying an academic subject, but vocational validating and examining bodies have given little encouragement to schemes that would enable students to take selected units of a vocational course in combination with academic studies.

Although academic programmes are less integrated than their vocational counterparts, the three A level package is so well established as the norm that most A level students automatically aspire to this as a recognised qualification level. Thus, in effect, they too are committed to a full-time package. This means that the majority of students in tertiary colleges, like their counterparts in other institutions, are specialising in either academic or vocational courses. The separateness of the two routes to qualification is accentuated by different timetable structures and patterns of work, so that students' lifestyles are determined more by their course than by their membership of the same institution. In order for students to benefit fully from the comprehensive provision of the tertiary college there needs to be a much more flexible mode of delivering both academic and vocational courses.

The nearest that institutions have come to a genuinely integrated course is the experimental combined A level/BTEC one-year foundation programme which has been made possible by modular approaches to A level. For example, the Gloucester College of Arts and Technology runs first-year science courses that provide joint accreditation in BTEC and Wessex modular A levels. A Brent initiative in three schools links the BTEC National Diploma in Business Studies and Finance with Cambridge modular A levels. Students who complete their first year successfully in these schemes are equipped to choose either the A level or vocational route to qualification in the second year. Such schemes emanate from dissatisfaction with a system that forces young people to make premature choices in their studies, often without the means for an informed decision.

THE INTEGRATION OF ACADEMIC AND VOCATIONAL EDUCATION

The government has announced its intention to raise the status of vocational work and will be introducing a new umbrella qualification in 1994 which, it is hoped, will help to establish parity between particular levels of vocational and academic achievement. The Advanced Diploma will be awarded to all students who gain NVQ level 3 qualifications or their GCE equivalent. What constitutes the academic equivalent of NVQ level 3 has been a matter of considerable conjecture and uncertainty. Current DFE thinking is that the Advanced Diploma should be awarded for passes in three A or AS subjects (one at least of which must be at A level) plus an appropriate level of competence, yet to be defined, in English, mathematics and a modern foreign language. The Diploma will also be given to those who achieve combined academic and vocational certification at the appropriate level.

The prejudices that afford such very different status to academic and vocational studies in this country are too deeply rooted to be much affected by strategies of this kind. The English respect for academic study is quite exceptional, amounting almost to reverence. By contrast, vocational education often has the image of basic instruction in low-level skills. Consequently many students, particularly those from upper- and middle-class homes, never attempt to inform themselves of the options open to them at 16+, but proceed more or less as a matter of course to an academic programme of study.

The low status of vocational courses stems largely from our total separation of the academic and vocational experiences and what C. P. Snow called our 'fanatical belief in educational specialisation'. We are inclined to regard working with one's hands and working with one's mind as separate activities and to assume that people are born with an aptitude for one or the other. For many years our educational system was organised to accommodate this view, children being classified and segregated at the age of 11 according to whether they were 'intelligent' or 'practical'. A further classification was attempted for a while – a group that came between the two basic species, the technically inclined and able.

There are still strong and influential advocates of such classification and segregation. In a Centre for Policy Studies publication, *End Egalitarian Delusion: Different Education for Different Talents*, Canon Pilkington, High Master of St Paul's, argues for schools to specialise in either academic or vocational courses:

> In particular, the paths followed by those pupils over 16 who wish to develop their academic gifts and those who wish to pursue their practical ones must be clearly signalled as different altogether.
>
> (Pilkington, 1991)

Post-16 colleges, like school sixth forms, should, he claims, specialise in either A/AS or vocational courses and probably be labelled 'Technical or Academic'.

It is only the right wing of the Conservative party that holds such views. However, as long as successive secretaries of state for education seek to preserve the sanctity of the traditional A level system, there will remain a doubt as to how seriously the government wishes to close the gap between academic and vocational courses. While the vocational curriculum is under-going constant change and improvement to meet current needs, its academic counterpart retains much of its outdated emphasis on content-based syllabuses, inflexible modes of delivery and restricted methods of assessment. In this situation, genuine integration of academic and vocational work remains extremely difficult, even when they are available under the same roof. Moreover, the constant eulogising of traditional A levels as the flagship of the English educational system, an internationally recognised gold standard of achievement, keeps up the pressure on the majority of young people to aspire to academic study and qualifications.

There is a growing view that the divisiveness of our educational system is the root cause of many of the problems of the 16–19 curriculum and that, until we abolish the barriers that exist between academic and vocational courses, our attempts at reform will continue to be ineffectual. This was the premise of the Institute for Public Policy Research report (1990). The IPPR suggested that strategies for improving the education of the 16–19 age group in this country have for too long concentrated on the particular weaknesses of the separate academic and vocational streams, instead of addressing the fundamental cause of the problems, the divided system itself:

> In our view, Britain's education system is marked by low 'staying-on' rates and poor comparative performance because it is *divided*. Most importantly, it divides 'academic' pupils from the rest through the different institutions, different curricula, different modes of study and above all different qualifications which cater for the two groups. Our qualifications system resembles an educational obstacle course and is designed to 'weed out' the majority of pupils. We call this the *early selection–low participation system*.
>
> Also, the unique structure of the labour market in Britain contributes to our educational failure. The labour market provides powerful incentives to early school learning. Full-time jobs, often in relatively well-paid and attractive occupations, encourage many 16 year olds, including the well quali-

fied, to leave school. Meanwhile, those who stay on in education to 18 may find they have missed out on training or career opportunities only open to younger leavers. Furthermore, the labour market fails to reward the acquisition of skills, especially the broad-based skills which new approaches to vocational education try to develop. By heightening the divisions in British education, the labour market sustains our incoherent 'mixed module' of 16–19 education and training.

(Institute for Public Policy Research, 1990)

The IPPR takes as its starting point for 16–19 curricular reform the abolition of the divisions between academic and vocational courses and argues that a more unified and inclusive system of education and training is required, both in the interests of a fairer society and the modern economy. A single 18+ qualification would replace the present dual system of academic and vocational certificates and diplomas with its 'debilitating divisions . . . between those selected to learn, those left to train, and those for whom education and training ends at 16'.

The new qualification, the British Baccalaureate, would cater for the interests, aptitudes and achievements of all students. To this end it would be based on a modular curriculum comprising a common core of content, skills and processes – and specialised choices. There would be three *domains* of study: social and human sciences; natural sciences and technology; arts, language and literature. Students would have considerable choice in compiling their programme of study but would take modules from each domain and pursue at least one area in greater depth. In addition to *core* and *specialist* modules there would be work experience/community-based elements. A more attractive and accessible 16+ curriculum would be matched by the removal of labour market incentives to early leaving, such as arbitrary age limits for entry to jobs. Subsidies for employer-led training would not be paid for young people until they were 18 and the Youth Training programme would be replaced by an 'education-led scheme' for young people leaving full-time education but without a job.

The idea of a single system of post-compulsory education has been widely debated and variations of the IPPR proposal recommended by two very different bodies: the Association of Principals of Sixth Form Colleges (APVIC) and the council of the Royal Society. The APVIC proposals (1991) called for an Advanced Diploma composed of units of study available at different levels, each separately graded and accredited, to produce programmes of varying depth and breadth. All students would take units from at least two curricular areas. A combination of units at an intermediate level could provide the basis for an Intermediate Diploma.

The Royal Society report, *Beyond GCSE* (1991), also proposed two qualifications, an Advanced Diploma (generally achieved after two years' full-time study) and an Advanced Certificate (generally achieved after one year of full-time study). Both qualifications would be gained by successful completion of a specified number of modules taken from three *domains* of study, similar to those advocated by the IPPR: social, economic and industrial; scientific, mathematical and technological; linguistic and aesthetic.

Both the APVIC and Royal Society proposals envisaged a gradual evolution from the present system, whereas the more radical IPPR recommendations were based on the abolition of the existing structure from the outset. All, however, sought the same long-term goal: the replacement of the present dual system of academic and vocational courses with a single broadly-based modular curriculum catering for the whole ability range. This objective has gained widespread support and was a keynote of a paper produced by the National Commission on Education in June 1992:

> There is no justification for dividing 16 year olds into two groups: those who only need to be educated, and those who only need to be trained. Moreover, neither academic nor vocational goals are efficiently achieved by separate and uncoordinated provision. Elements of both academic and vocational education should be incorporated in the curriculum of every student . . .
>
> (National Commission on Education, 1992)

Chapter 5

General education

BREADTH AND BALANCE IN THE 16–19 STUDENT EXPERIENCE

There is an obvious ambivalence in our educational aims and objectives with respect to the 16–19 age group. As earlier chapters have indicated, the traditional specialist approach to 16+ certification is extremely resistant to change. Yet the need to provide a broad and balanced student experience is widely recognised.

Throughout our school system there is a strong commitment to Renaissance principles, to the idea of developing fully rounded individuals, generally well-educated members of society. Having spent much time and energy pursuing this ideal during the years of compulsory schooling, we are constantly questioning the wisdom of discarding it at 16. Schools and colleges have sought to resolve this dilemma in two ways: by offering a range of extra-curricular activities and by designing a non-examined curriculum to broaden students' study programmes.

EXTRA-CURRICULAR PROVISION

The extra-curricular dimension to school life is an important part of the English tradition of education. The boarding school, in particular, has always sought to provide pupils with a whole way of life, occupying their time not only with classes and prep, but with numerous broadening and character-building activities: sport, training for the armed forces, music, drama, a range of clubs and societies. Sixth formers have not merely participated in these activities, but played a major part in running them. Indeed it has been through its extra-curricular provision that the public school has provided most of its training for the leadership roles that many of its pupils will aspire to in later life.

The day school cannot expect to emulate the high participation rate in extra-curricular activities achieved by most boarding schools. However, many day schools, private and maintained, offer an extensive programme of activities during lunch-hours, after school and on Saturday mornings. There are considerable variations in these programmes. The influence of the prestigious public schools is strong, particularly in the independent schools and state grammar schools, even to the extent of their adopting a 'house system' as a vehicle for inter-group sporting contests and other competitions. The greater the emphasis a school places on academic competition the more likely it is to encourage team games. The progressive independent schools, on the other hand, play down competition in favour of individual sports and creative and cultural opportunities. As a general rule, comprehensive schools place less emphasis than selective schools on team games and other opportunities for competition. Alternatives include a range of outdoor activities and community service programmes, the latter being particularly well-developed in some of the neighbourhood comprehensives.

Sixth form and tertiary colleges provide extensive extra-curricular activities which benefit greatly from the large number of older students concentrated in one community. This applies particularly to musical, dramatic and sporting activities, and the standard of orchestras, choirs, team games and drama productions can be very high. These activities are staff-run, but the students assume considerable responsibility for much of the extra-curricular life of the colleges, particularly the publication of magazines and newspapers and the organisation of social and fund-raising events. In FE colleges such matters are often left almost entirely to the student union, much as in Higher Education. In sixth form colleges, and often in tertiary, there is a staff presence, albeit operating in a supportive and advisory rather than a management role. Some of the colleges' social and fund-raising events can become major occasions involving the whole institution and generating a strong community feeling.

THE DEVELOPMENT OF GENERAL STUDIES

General studies originated in some modest attempts by both independent and maintained schools to broaden the curricular demands on sixth formers beyond their examination courses. An early form of general course was the weekly discussion group led by headmasters and headmistresses in the post-war years. The chosen topics owed much to Oxbridge high-table conversation pieces – philosophy, religion, moral issues, current affairs. Elsewhere the subject approach was adopted, with students being required to spend one or two periods a week on English, religion and perhaps a foreign language. There were other combinations, civics and music being frequent components. The programmes were heavily arts dominated.

The 1959 Crowther Report, *15–18*, commented on the inadequacy of these arrangements, observing that they were rarely taken very seriously by staff and, inevitably therefore, by sixth formers. In particular, they did little 'to make science students more literate' and 'nothing to make arts specialists more numerate'. Heads and sixth form teachers were well aware of the shortcomings of 'minority-time' studies, with their 'useful way of filling a wet Friday afternoon' image. Response to the Crowther Report's criticisms, and to the two-culture debate initiated by C. P. Snow in the same year, tended therefore to be quite positive. In 1961, following Peterson's Oxford conferences on the sixth form curriculum, 360 heads of independent and maintained schools signed an Agreement to Broaden the Curriculum (ABC) pledging themselves to meet Crowther's recommendation that nine or ten periods in a 35-period week should be devoted to non-specialist studies, in addition to games. This movement was given added impetus with the formation of the General Studies Association in 1963.

The general studies movement took a firm hold and by 1969 the Schools' Council was able to comment on 'the achievement and example of many schools' in pioneering effective sixth form general studies. Whilst by no means all schools achieved the target of over 25 per cent timetable provision, by the late 1960s most sixth forms had significantly enhanced their general studies programmes. In the absence of any major change in the specialist approach to examination work, general studies have thus become the main way in which schools and colleges have provided breadth and variety in the 16–19 curriculum.

THE VARIETY OF GENERAL STUDIES PROVISION

There is no consensus over what constitutes general studies. One of their attractions is that they are an area of the curriculum over which institutions can exercise freedom of choice. Programmes consequently owe much to the ingenuity and imagination of particular schools and colleges and to individual teachers within them. There are many variations of emphasis and approach, both between institutions and also between the different components of the more ambitious programmes.

The traditions of the selective sixth form are maintained in those options that seek to stimulate intellectual curiosity and encourage wide reading and debate. Such courses may be subject-based or of a more general nature; for example, a science-in-society discussion group for arts students or a broadly-based arts course for scientists. Some schools and colleges run cross-curricular general discussion groups; papers may be delivered on a range of topics by students and staff.

The influence of the old Oxbridge common entrance and GCE Scholarship (S level) papers is strong here and this approach to general studies has been encapsulated in the GCE A level general studies examination. First introduced in 1959, this subject is now the third most popular A level, its 1992 candidature of 47,000 being exceeded only by that of English and mathematics. The great majority of A level general studies candidates take the Joint Matriculation Board (JMB) examination and come from schools and colleges in the north. Whilst the Board assumes that its centres will run classes specifically geared to the examination, it is careful to recognise that schools and colleges 'attach great importance to their freedom to construct their own courses of General Studies, and that the content of courses will vary widely in accordance with the needs of students' (JMB, 1992). Emphasis is placed on candidates' extending their own general education by 'discussion, reading (including the reading of newspapers) and by taking advantage of opportunities available through school activities, radio and television, theatres, concerts and the like'.

In accordance with this policy, A level general studies examination questions range widely across different disciplines and issues, discouraging the narrowly focused preparation that can sometimes stultify the teaching and learning process in specialist subjects. Nevertheless, the purists argue that general studies should not be examined, indeed that, by its very nature, general education cannot be prescribed and confined in a way that enables valid comparisons to be made between students on the basis of selective examination questions.

An early alternative to examined general studies was the programme of hobby courses through which teachers sought to convey their enthusiasm for a variety of personal interests, ranging from archaeology to bird-watching, photography to wine-making. The aim was to provide a complete change from the examined curriculum and to arouse young people's interest in a potentially rewarding leisure-time activity. This form of general study survives, but has declined in popularity. The hobby course has a somewhat staid and elderly image and it is difficult to maintain the interest of the non-enthusiast.

The freedom to design one's own course brings with it the problem of finding or producing sufficiently relevant high quality materials. It is not as easy for publishers to target the general studies market as it is to provide textbooks for standard examination syllabuses. There have, however, been some imaginative attempts to design materials on which to base general studies courses. The Schools Council/York University packs on sociological, political and moral themes and topics did much to influence non-examination social science courses in the 1970s and the Science and Technology in Society (SATIS) materials published by the Association for Science Education (ASE) are currently enjoying a similar vogue.

In general, however, there has been a move away from resource-based studies to more active forms of student participation. Given the importance that our society and educational system place on examination success and certification, it is always hard work arousing and maintaining student interest in the non-examined curriculum. The task, however, is made easier, and indeed more credible, if general studies provide a break from the academic intensity of examination work. Students welcome a change in style as well as content.

To this extent the thinking behind the hobby course has prevailed: that general studies ought to provide a totally different type of learning experience from that of the examination course. Thus there has been a steady growth in creative and practical courses and a much greater emphasis on student involvement. Schools and colleges have sought opportunities to get students out of the classroom and off site for various forms of project work and field studies, for work experience and community service. Case studies, simulation exercises and business games have become popular, particularly as a means of heightening economic awareness. Computer literacy, word-processing and other information technology courses are well established. Such initiatives are an indication of the way in which general studies are seen as the part of the curriculum that can most readily respond to the demands of post-16 Technical and Vocational Education Extension (TVEE) and the pressure for an element of vocational work to be included in all students' programmes.

STRATEGIES FOR PROVIDING A GENERAL STUDIES PROGRAMME

The diversification of general studies provision has increased the logistic problems facing the small 16–19 unit. The comprehensive school sixth form has a particular dilemma. The mixed ability intake requires a wide range of non-examination options just as it does of examination courses and this has been a contributory factor in the changing pattern of general studies. On the other hand, in all but the largest comprehensive school sixth forms, it is extremely difficult to resource and timetable an extensive programme of non-examination options. Invariably the first priority is seen to be the provision of an adequate range of examination courses.

Few institutions can do everything that they would like to do to further students' general education, but the larger colleges, with their flexibility of timetabling and greater resources, normally offer a comprehensive programme that reflects the variety of activities now encompassed by the term general studies. Sixth form colleges usually require a level of commitment to this aspect of the curriculum amounting to at least a fifth of a student's programme of study, perhaps with some reduction in the second year. This may include or be in addition to games and recreational activities.

Some colleges have a single general studies programme that

includes all types of course, from which students make a free or guided choice. Where an element of negotiation enters into the arrangements the aim is usually to encourage breadth and balance in a student's total programme of examination and non-examination work. Other colleges introduce an element of prescription with a programme that combines a compulsory core and a range of electives. Most typically, the core consists of a course of personal and social education, including such elements as study skills, political and moral issues, health, sex and careers education. This course may be taught by a team of staff brought together for the purpose. The trend, though, is in favour of these elements being delivered as a tutorial package by all staff who have a personal tutoring responsibility.

The electives part of such dual programmes varies in its emphasis and rationale from institution to institution, as evidenced by the different names given to this aspect of the curriculum: entitlement, enhancement, enterprise; extension or alternative studies; complementary or supplementary studies; interest courses or liberal studies. Some programmes are composed of one-year courses, but shorter units and modular approaches are popular. Most TVEE-initiated courses are part of an electives system, but some are finding their way into core or tutorial packages. Equal opportunities and economic awareness components are examples. Other popular options or electives include information technology; extra support for students with weaknesses in basic subjects; workshops in English as a foreign language and English as a second language; preparation for specific careers such as teaching and nursing; and the Duke of Edinburgh Award Scheme and outward-bound activities. Creative and practical courses figure prominently and are sometimes given a separate timetable slot, perhaps as an alternative to games.

Some colleges make a feature of conferences, activity days, theme weeks, programmes of lead-lectures, visiting speakers, workshops run by writers/artists in residence and young enterprise schemes. These may be occasional initiatives or regular events.

Institutions have set their own standards of general studies provision: there has been no external evaluation beyond occasional HMI or LEA adviser/inspector interest. The courses stand or fall on the quality of their design and delivery, that is on the ability, imagination and enthusiasm of individual members of staff. Students who will tolerate interminable boredom on an examination course quickly vote with their feet on an unsuccessful non-examination course. The ultimate test of general studies is the attendance level in the latter stages of the course. The quality of provision varies greatly from institution to institution, and within institutions. The Crowther Report's criticism that these studies are often not taken seriously by staff or students remains as true today as it was over 30 years ago. Nevertheless, the richness of provision in some schools and colleges and the high quality of particular courses in many others are a constant reminder of teachers' resourcefulness in compensating for the narrowness of 16–19 examination study programmes.

THE FE LIBERAL STUDIES MOVEMENT

FE colleges have bred their own particular reaction to over-specialisation. The early tradition of general education for vocational course students was not dissimilar to that for their academic counterparts, but there are significant differences in the way it has developed. A liberal education movement gained momentum in the expanding post-war colleges to counteract the limited educational experience offered by vocational courses. It was led by enthusiasts who believed fervently that there is in every human being a longing, however latent, for something more from life than the mere satisfaction of elemental needs and that 'a technical education properly conceived and conducted should be no less a liberal education than the studies trad-itionally followed elsewhere' (DES, 1957). Official recognition of the movement led to courses being run by the Cambridge Board of Extra Mural Studies and the formation in the early 1960s of an Association of Liberal Education.

Within a college, FE liberal studies lecturers constituted a small, closely-knit team crusading for an educational ideal rarely shared by the staff as a whole. In schools and sixth form colleges a considerable number of staff have been involved in the teaching of general studies, but each person's commitment has been relatively small in timetable terms. By contrast, in FE colleges the majority of staff were untouched by the liberal studies movement, but the team of staff who were committed to this work spent the majority or even the whole of their time teaching the liberal studies component of students' programmes. Thus liberal/ general studies have enjoyed a broader base and wider support in the schools sector, but had a more identifiable focal point and coherent philosophy in FE.

General studies teaching has always been hard work. It was particularly so in FE colleges where respect for the specialist's mastery of a particular expertise is even greater than in the academic field. Moreover, for students whose purpose in continuing with their full-time education is to obtain a vocational training and qualification the relevance of liberal studies is far from obvious. Hence the caricatured lecturer in Tom Sharpe's novel, *Wilt*, struggling to interest Gasfitters 3 in the emotional significance of the interpersonal relationships in *Sons and Lovers*.

THE INTEGRATION OF VOCATIONAL TRAINING AND GENERAL EDUCATION

The lack of any direct connection between most liberal studies courses and students' specialist vocational training led to a shift in emphasis in the general education of most FE students. As early as 1962 a Ministry of Education publication, *General Studies in Technical Colleges*, gave particular emphasis to the importance of helping students solve problems of communication. In 1970 a City and Guilds committee placed communication first in a list of general studies aims and subsequently pursued this priority with increasing enthusiasm.

Until this point the FE examining and validating bodies had been little involved in the liberal studies movement. However, in 1975 the Technician Education Council (TEC) introduced a general and communication studies module into its courses which carried 15 per cent of the marks in the final assessment. From its inception in 1974 the Business Education Council (BEC) had a system of problem-solving cross-modular assignments in communication built into all its courses. Many liberal studies enthusiasts were sceptical of these formalised and functional roles for general studies. Others, tired of trying to inculcate middle-class values in craft apprentices, had already moved in the direction of process-based courses. These lecturers welcomed a move that they considered gave increased status to their part of the FE curriculum.

When the TEC and BEC merged in 1983 the BEC model of cross-curricular assignments became predominant. BTEC courses at all levels (First, National and Higher National) stress the importance of a range of common skills and core themes designed to develop the general personal competences that make the difference between success and failure at work.

In a 1991 review of policy on the general component of its vocational courses, BTEC identified seven important common skills:

- managing and developing self
- working with and relating to others
- communicating
- managing tasks and solving problems
- applying numeracy
- applying technology
- applying design and creativity.

Parallel developments have taken place in other vocational courses so that examined transferable skills have become the general education component in the vocational curriculum. The clearly-defined role ascribed to common skills in the new-style vocational courses has raised the status of certain aspects of general education and broadened the nature of examination work. These benefits have to be weighed against the loss of a liberal education element in students' programmes of study. The price paid for an enhanced role for general education is the acceptance of a narrower interpretation of what that concept means.

CORE SKILLS ACROSS THE CURRICULUM

The late 1980s saw the development of a core skills movement in schools and sixth form colleges that closely paralleled the common skills development in the vocational curriculum. Encouraged through various post-16 TVE Initiatives this movement initially impinged only on the non-examined curriculum. However, in 1989, following a succession of reports calling for common learning outcomes for all learners over 16, John MacGregor, the then Secretary of State for Education and

Science, asked the NCC, in consultation with SEAC, NCVQ, the Further Education Unit and the then Training Agency, to recommend a set of core skills that could be defined and incorporated into the study programmes of students aged 16–19 taking A/AS courses. In its response in March 1990 the NCC proposed that the following list of skills should be incorporated into the study programmes of all students aged 16–19:

Group 1	Group 2
Communication	Numeracy
Problem-solving	Information technology
Personal skills	Modern foreign language competence

SEAC considered that the first group of skills could form part of the assessed work in all A/AS syllabuses. It would be possible to embed aspects of numeracy and information technology in appropriate syllabuses. The foreign language would have to be a separate component of the post-16 entitlement. The NCVQ came out strongly in support of the NCC list of core skills and recommended that attainment in the first group of transferable core skills – communication, problem-solving, personal skills – should be included in all NVQs, with increasing degrees of competence required at each level. During 1991, a joint initiative involving NCC, SEAC, NCVQ and FEU developed definitions for the NCC core skills at four levels of attainment. These agreed definitions have formed the basis for separate exemplification exercises by SEAC and NCVQ, designed to determine the extent to which core skills could be embedded in NVQs and A/AS syllabuses and how they might be assessed for certification purposes.

The core skills movement has brought together the various bodies responsible for academic and vocational courses and contributed to the development of the view that the 16–19 curriculum should be regarded as an entity. The apparent consensus over the common ground does however conceal significant differences in the extent to which academic and vocational courses are receptive to the concept of transferable core skills. The vocational curriculum has taken important steps in this direction during the last decade and each of the main examining bodies has a coherent policy on the general component of specialist qualifications. The situation with regard to A level syllabuses is, however, much more variable. Because of the control exerted by the GCE boards' separate subject panels, the rate and extent of syllabus reform varies from subject to subject within, as well as between, boards.

Some A level syllabuses remain little affected by forty years of change in 16–19 education: like their higher school certificate predecessors they consist of a restricted list of study topics and factual information to be learnt for a terminal written examination. Others require not merely a knowledge of factual information but an understanding of a subject's essential processes through which students can learn a variety of specialist and general skills. Most subject syllabuses are in a transitional stage – still heavily content-based, but recognising the need to provide better progression from the more varied learning experiences encouraged by GCSE and to explore ways of assessing students' understanding of process as well as their knowledge of subject matter. There are increasing attempts to improve students' powers of written and oral comprehension and communication and their skills of investigation, experimentation and problem-solving.

The core skills development is changing the emphasis of 16–19 general education, but with significantly different effects on the academic and vocational curriculum. With the integration of general skills into examined courses the vocational curriculum has abandoned the separate non-examined general studies component and with it the liberal education ideal. The slower, more uneven development of core skills as an integrated part of academic courses has prompted schools and colleges to provide specific opportunities for skills acquisition, both in the form of certificated courses, in, for example, word-processing and computing, and as additions to their non-examined general studies provision. Core skills and their partner, cross-curricular themes, have added further dimensions to an already diversified programme of supporting courses in which liberal studies remain an important component.

The difference in the way in which we provide for the general education of those following academic and vocational courses is, to some extent, the consequence of the different methods by which their programmes are structured, the one being a collection of separate subjects, the other a unified package. At the same time, it owes something to the two-species theory and the assumptions made about the different needs of two categories of student, as exemplified in long-standing conflicts between the two government departments concerned with education and training – the DFE and the DoE.

Chapter 6

The learning experience

TEACHER-CENTRED EDUCATION

The nature of the curriculum inevitably influences the way in which it is delivered. The traditional specialist approach to 16–19 education and training in this country permeates the whole system – the syllabuses, the courses, the teaching methods, the student's learning experience.

Specialisms are a means of classifying knowledge and experience and of developing a high level of expertise in one area of human activity. They are concerned with specific aspects of human endeavour and achievement, different vantage points on the world and its inhabitants. Each specialism has generated its own body of knowledge, concepts, skills, even its own distinctive language.

The uniqueness of a specialist subject, profession or trade is carefully cultivated and preserved. Before one can even begin a specialist course of study or training one has to meet certain entry requirements, usually in the form of academic qualifications, which may or may not be directly relevant to the course for which one has applied. The route to certification can be long and arduous and the drop-out rate high. The final examination leads to the rejection of a percentage of those who have completed the course, sometimes as many as a third or more. Eventual qualification inevitably brings a sense of exclusive membership and status.

The further one takes specialist study or training the more narrowly focused the work becomes; and, the more specific the field of expertise, the more highly regarded the specialist. The orthopaedist or neurologist is held in greater esteem than the GP,

the heating or sanitary engineer is a cut above the all-purpose plumber. The single honours degree ranks higher than a combined or general degree. 'Jack of all trades' is a derogatory term.

The exclusivity of the specialism is self-perpetuating. It is taught by qualified experts who have been immersed in the traditions of their unique branch of human knowledge. The majority are enthusiasts, keen to pass on to the next generation the feelings of achievement they have gained from the mastery of their specialism.

Thus the relationship between teacher and student, trainer and trainee, is that of expert and initiate. The initial points of contact between the two are very few. From the outset, then, the obvious teaching and learning strategy is for the teacher/trainer to inform and instruct, and for the student/trainee to listen and carry out instructions. It is very difficult to change this relationship. As the learner acquires knowledge and skill, so the pace and difficulty of the work increase, thereby maintaining, or appearing to maintain, the need for a didactic approach.

Imparting one's knowledge to people who are relatively uninformed is an enjoyable experience. It is often said that teachers are actors at heart and certainly most of them enjoy giving a performance. Some become extremely good at it. Many of us can recall a great pedagogue from our own schooldays to whose charisma and enthusiasm we attribute the early stirrings of our own love of learning. Teachers who are able to transmit knowledge, understanding and enthusiasm by their sheer personality and presentation skills have a very special gift. They should use it generously, but it will be all the more effective if it is not the only teaching method they employ.

Not all teachers are gifted lecturers. Most, however, acquire a degree of confidence and feeling of security in the role, which then becomes self-perpetuating. The formalities inherent in the didactic method facilitate order and discipline: the teacher is very much in control of proceedings and feels a continual sense of achievement and satisfaction from exercising pedagogic and managerial authority.

Few teachers today use the authority of their position in a domineering or intimidating way, as often happened in the past. The relationship with the 16+ age group is particularly friendly and relaxed: students are encouraged to ask questions, contribute ideas, seek individual help. In practical work they usually have considerable freedom of access to equipment and other members of the class. Nevertheless, the standard teaching method with 16+ students is still largely didactic. One has only to take a five-minute walk round any college or sixth form teaching block to realise the extent to which the work is teacher-dominated.

This situation owes more to expediency than ideology. Teachers are generally agreed that the ultimate aim of the formal education process must be to enable students to assume responsibility for their own learning and they appreciate that, to achieve this, students have to become actively engaged in the essential processes of the subjects they study. There is, however, a day-to-day pragmatism that works in the reverse direction. Strong forces militate against the use of methods designed to foster student independence. Teachers cite, in particular, overlarge classes, inadequate resources and insufficient time.

The time factor is especially significant. The importance of tradition in specialist subjects makes it difficult to change their well-established core of content, with the result that in any updating of syllabuses, additions tend to outweigh deletions. Teachers of both academic and vocational courses complain constantly of overloading of syllabuses and the consequent constraints on the way in which courses are delivered. Unless teachers keep tight control of the content and pace of each period of contact time, they feel they will not 'get through the syllabus'. 'Getting through the syllabus' is a high priority in a society that attaches so much importance to examination results.

The non-didactic approach to teaching – putting students at the centre of the learning process – creates a fluid and unpredictable teaching context. The teacher has to be prepared for all kinds of unforeseen situations, peripheral questions, individual interpretations and new applications of syllabus content. Starting from the student's sphere of awareness shifts the whole perspective of a subject from the past to the present, so that the teacher must always be right up to date.

Didactic teaching enables one to make set-piece presentations on specific syllabus topics, perfected through repetition over a number of years. The conscientious and able practitioner will, of course, make regular adjustments to accommodate current developments and different classes. The degree of adaptability required, however, in orchestrating a continually open-ended classroom situation calls for personal and management skills of a special order. Not surprisingly many teachers choose the easier option.

Assessment procedures exert one of the strongest influences on teaching methods, and A level examination conventions have been a major factor in perpetuating the didactic method of delivering academic courses. For many years the standard terminal written assessment of A level work has concentrated on a subject's theoretical and historical base, not on its modern applications. It has tested a facility to recall facts rather than to handle process and been concerned more with knowledge than understanding. The temptation has thus been to spoonfeed students with the information they need to satisfy the examiner in a competitive, norm-referenced test. Generations of students have acquiesced in this exercise and come to share their teachers' primary concern to get through the syllabus. In the process many have learnt to be suspicious of any deviation from the set material, any lesson that leaves them without revision notes, any situation that throws them back on their own resources.

STUDENT-CENTRED EDUCATION

There have always been educators who have fiercely resisted this syndrome. They have believed, as Aristotle did, that we learn from doing and that the role of the teacher is to set up the situations and provide the opportunities for students' own active learning. Teacher and learner become partners in a shared experience. The student is at the centre: the teacher acts as tutor, consultant, mentor.

This view is diametrically opposed to the thinking that has traditionally underpinned further and higher education in this country. The active learner is seen not as an unquestioning recipient of received wisdom, but as a potential contributor to the search for new truths. Thus we learn of the notions and methodologies of the past in order to assess their relevance to the present. We seek knowledge of a subject in order to understand the world around us. We memorise those basic facts that we require daily but, more importantly, learn how to access a much greater store of knowledge in order to extract the information we need for specific purposes. Education is ultimately about the acquisition of skills that enable us to conceptualise, make judgements, solve problems, think creatively and communicate.

It is a process that begins in the early stages of schooling but which frequently stultifies in the post-16 sector.

Teachers of A level who believe in this liberating view of education are in a difficult situation. Even the most flexible syllabus available to them may impose constraints on the pursuit of their ideals. Ultimately their frustration may drive them into syllabus design and the politics of curricular reform. During the 1970s and 1980s teachers were able to exert some influence over the curriculum through membership of the advisory committees of the examination boards and successive national bodies responsible for curriculum development – the Schools Council for Curriculum and Examinations (1965–1984), the School Examinations Council (1984–1988) and the School Examinations and Assessment Council (1988 to date). It has also been possible for groups of teachers and LEA advisers to submit proposals for new syllabuses to these bodies via the examination boards.

These developments have been largely uncoordinated and piecemeal, influencing different boards and different specialisms to varying degrees. Modern foreign language syllabuses and teaching have been the most affected. In the early 1970s modern language teaching was firmly rooted in the detailed study of literary texts from the past. The courses were relevant only to a small number of candidates hoping to proceed to honours degree courses in foreign literature. Now they are concerned with the development of comprehension and communication skills tested through a variety of oral, aural and written responses to the language. The student experience comprises a wide range of activities relating to the language as it is spoken and written today. The classes are invariably conducted in the foreign language and the materials drawn from a variety of modern contexts. The courses are relevant to students proceeding to many different HE options and also to those going straight into employment at 18.

New syllabuses being introduced in other subjects show similar changes. The traditional narrow focus on students' recall facility is giving way to a much wider range of demands: conceptual understanding in addition to factual knowledge; an acquaintance with modern processes and applications as well as past theories; an acquisition of skills of investigation, problem-solving, presentation and communication. Where this transition is complete, the teacher no longer has to teach to the examination, students being assessed not on prescribed material or routine exercises, but through a series of previously unseen tasks designed to test the skills they have acquired on the course. The following extract from the Welsh Joint Examinations Council (WJEC) craft, design and technology syllabus illustrates the implications of this change:

> The problems set will aim at assessing ability to handle and evaluate given information, the resourcefulness in applying previous experience to a new situation, and the ingenuity, originality and inventiveness displayed in tackling open-ended problems. Questions requiring only technical information for their solution will not be set. When such information is required it will be made available to the candidate. It is not intended that candidates prepare for specific problems by rote-learning.
>
> (WJEC, 1989)

Such approaches remain the exception rather than the rule, but the pace of change has quickened as traditional A level syllabuses have come in for increasing criticism following major changes to the 14–16 curriculum. The TVE Initiative and TVE Extension have related the school experience more closely to the workplace and raised the status of practical and technical activities. The GCSE has introduced more varied assessment procedures and methods of course delivery. These initiatives have increased student motivation and encouraged more to continue with their education beyond the age of 16. The expectations raised have, however, not always been fulfilled, and the mismatch between the new approaches in the 14–16 sector and traditional A level courses has emphasised the arid and out-of-date nature of much post-16 work.

Committees, working-parties and networks set up to enable teachers to work on the new 14–16 courses have often remained in existence to develop a 14–19 continuum. Some of these groups have been concerned with specific subjects: the Hampshire GCSE Business Information Studies, for example, led naturally to the design of a BIS A level. Other groups have engaged in more ambitious schemes to change the nature of A level courses across the whole curriculum.

The modular experience

A number of initiatives in different parts of the country have sought to modularise A level courses. The most successful of these has been the Wessex project, produced by a consortium of west country LEAs in conjunction with the Associated Examining Board (AEB). The aim of this project was to develop in one part of an A level syllabus approaches similar to those that have proved successful in the GCSE, while retaining the traditional prescribed core content in the other. The 60 per cent core is taught over the normal two years and assessed mainly by means of a final examination set by the GCE board. The teaching of the core is, however, suspended at regular intervals to enable students to work intensively on a practical project which they choose themselves from a bank of modules. Each A level requires a student to complete four of these modules over the two years, a single module accounting for 10 per cent of the final marks for the course.

Staff and students working on Wessex A levels are enthusiastic about the approach. An independent survey established that the modules were considered more accessible, relevant and interesting than traditional courses. The modular approach and its regular assessment give an immediacy to the work. The pressure points of the course are evenly spaced and the structure encourages consistent application. The variety of learning situations and assessment procedures widens the range of demands on students; different types of task reveal their different strengths.

Although the common core part of the course suffers by comparison with the modules, there has been some extension of the methods used with the modules into the core. Despite the usual pressure to get through the prescribed syllabus content, staff are more confident in transferring responsibility to students for sections of the core content because of their experience of the modular approach.

The first Wessex A level was in chemistry in 1987, followed a year later by physics and biology. Other syllabuses were designed and there is now a total of ten accepted by SEAC on a trial basis. There are two other well-publicised modular schemes. The Cambridge modular bank was the outcome of a Cambridge TVEI project involving four counties: Cambridgeshire, Bedfordshire, Northamptonshire and Hertfordshire. It was launched to provide continuity from the 14–16 TVEI and to preserve the spirit of joint enterprise between institutions in the TVEI consortium. There was a strong commitment to a teaching and learning structure with short-term objectives that supported active learning and problem-solving methods. Courses consist of six modules for A level, three for AS, and there are some double modules. Syllabuses have been designed in twelve subjects. The Ridgeway modular scheme was devised by the Ridgeway School in Swindon to provide progression from GCSE approaches and as a strategy for introducing AS levels. In the Wessex and Cambridgeshire schemes students choose their modules; in the Ridgeway scheme there is some choice for AS students but none for A level.

There are various degrees of modularity and considerable differences in the way the strategy is interpreted and applied. Modules may simply be a structural device for breaking a course down into manageable units; students may have no choice of topic and the teaching style may be unaffected by the way the course is structured. Most advocates of the system, however, see modularity as a way of putting students at the centre of the learning process, recognising the way in which they are motivated by short-term goals and regular assessment, crediting them for what they achieve as the course progresses, giving them a choice of subject matter and greater responsibility for organising and pacing their work.

The modular curriculum is also seen by many educationists as the ultimate strategy for broadening 16–19 studies. If all courses consisted of a number of self-contained, separately assessed units, it would be possible for students to compile a programme to suit their individual needs and interests. They could range as widely as they liked across different parts of the curriculum, including both academic and vocational components.

SEAC has consistently advised modular course-designers not to go down this path. Even modest proposals by the Wessex and Cambridge projects to combine modules from closely-allied subject areas have met with strong resistance. Clearly the council has seen no future for a 'pick and mix' approach to modular courses when the government has so unequivocally rejected less radical proposals for broadening the curriculum, such as the five-subject programme advocated by the Higginson Committee.

Experiencing general education through the specialist course

An inherent weakness of the separate subject curriculum is its lack of cohesion. Even with an A level programme made up of, for example, physics, chemistry and mathematics, students are almost invariably left to make the connections between the separate subjects for themselves. It is only the very able who can do this effectively. The more subjects or modules one takes, the more fragmented and incohesive the programme risks becoming. Indeed there is an irony in all attempts to broaden the 16–19 academic curriculum by increasing the number of discrete specialisms. The pressure upon the teacher to impart essential information about the specialism in the limited time available usually precludes attempts to deal with general applications and to explore links between the different elements of a student's programme.

In the 1960s most of the Maidstone Grammar School Arts Sixth were persuaded to restrict their A levels to two, on the grounds that a more leisurely, broadly-based pursuit of two subjects was likely to provide a better general education than a narrower more intensive application to the syllabuses of three. Students were remarkably well read. On the English Literature course, for example, the first two terms were spent encouraging wide reading and discussing many different styles and periods of literature, before beginning the traditional detailed textual analysis of works prescribed by the examination board.

There have always been teachers who have argued, perhaps somewhat tongue in cheek, that their particular specialist subject encapsulates the whole of human experience. Imaginative teaching certainly has the power to turn a specialist course into a first-rate general education. The transformation is easier to achieve, though, in an arts subject like English or history than in, say, A level chemistry or a vocational course in engineering. The Maidstone Grammar School policy was not extended to the science sixth, but then that option was not available since a science qualification restricted to two subjects would have denied students admission to university. Yet if one considers the possibilities for a chemistry department given, for example, double the time to cover its present A level syllabus, or the same allocation of time for a syllabus consisting of half the customary content, the potential for general education is considerable.

Imagine, for example, a major project entailing an extended placement in a pharmaceutical firm co-tutored by a teacher and an industrialist. Students could study some of the medical challenges presented to the research and development unit and the resulting interaction between the biologists who analyse the problems and the chemists who seek to invent the drugs that overcome them. They could follow the whole development process through the testing of possibilities and choice of a product, then consider the mathematical probability of success and the economic factors that have to be taken into account. When the project came to consider the manufacturing and marketing processes, students could look at the engineering implications of the equipment and packaging required and the role of various departments such as personnel and publicity. They could study the literature produced in relation to the product, the ethical issues involved in its marketing and the insurance costs incurred in protecting the firm should users of the drug experience unforeseen side-effects.

Having studied the context in which chemical knowledge contributes to a process involving many other branches of knowledge and human skills, students might then each select a problem-solving exercise as a special project. For potential chemists this would undoubtedly be a chemistry problem, such as how to produce a tablet hard enough to stand up to the manufacturing process but able to dissolve in use. But others might choose an engineering problem – why a tablet compression machine is unable to run at full speed without constantly breaking down, or how to develop a by-pass system in a conveyor belt in order to isolate a fault and so maintain production during repairs. Other possibilities might be to look at marketing, moral and economic issues arising from a competitor's producing a similar product, or a personnel problem such as smoking policy in a firm with a high health awareness, or policy in dealing with the media during the firm's involvement in a court case.

The involvement in the real world that this kind of project gives students is a very strong motivator. Their theoretical studies acquire meaning. They see the significance of their specialism in a working context and become aware of its relationship to other specialist branches of knowledge. They begin to appreciate something of the complexity of human relationships. Above all, they engage in problem-solving, decision-making activities that have an obvious relevance to the world in which people live and work. They may indeed find themselves involved in real as opposed to hypothetical situations, helping to solve actual problems that exist at the time of their placement and experiencing the satisfaction and exhilaration of contributing to a solution that increases profits, eases relations between management and workforce, or improves working conditions in some way.

The general studies experience

The ultimate learning experience is not the simulation exercise or case study, invaluable as these are: it is participating in real situations. During the late 1970s and 1980s Queen Mary's College in Basingstoke shifted the emphasis of its extensive main (non-examined) studies programme from resource-based discussion topics to more practical activities – outward bound and young enterprise options, business-related courses with work experience components, problem-solving and project-based courses in design, creative writing workshops and practical music-making, and a number of services to the college and wider community.

A particularly ambitious project was the development of an arts centre based on new accommodation provided for the 200 students following courses in drama and music. Programmed by the drama and music departments, the college's Central Studio added a new dimension to the region's arts provision, catering for the student age group and a wide range of minority interests – early English music, jazz, modern dance, fringe theatre, poetry, the music and drama of other cultures.

The studio was run by staff and students who managed the box office and all the front-of-house activities, including a small refreshment bar. Two student technical crews serviced an extensive programme of student recitals, concerts and plays. Students wrote the scripts, composed the music, made the costumes and designed the sets for all their dramatic events. Interspersed with these student activities were masterclasses, workshops and performances by professional musicians, dance companies and theatre groups. The programme eventually occupied a hundred evenings a year and attracted sponsorship from the borough and county council, local industry and the Southern Arts Association. The Central Studio is now part of a much larger college/community liaison exercise, the Regional Centre, which attempts to link all parts of the college curriculum with local interest groups through an extra-mural programme of seminars, talks, conferences, exhibitions, workshops and special events.

One of the most successful links between Queen Mary's College and the town it serves has been Grapevine, a project emanating from a non-examination computer course that provides the 80,000 inhabitants of Basingstoke with a 10,000-item videotext information service available at twelve access points in the town. Students research and key-in information on every aspect of the region's amenities and services from restaurant prices to bus and train times, playgroups to cinema and theatre programmes. The text is updated daily and provides an ongoing commitment with real outcomes, the significance and import-ance of which are obvious to the students on the course.

Both the Central Studio and Grapevine became successful business ventures consuming many hours of staff and student time outside the normal working day. Eventually salaried staff had to be employed to reduce the workload of the teaching staff and students most heavily involved – a full-time administrator for Grapevine and an administrator, technician and part-time secretary and wardrobe mistress for the Central Studio. Several of the people appointed to these posts were ex-students who had been among the pioneers who set up the projects.

The added dimension of salaried staff provided opportunities for growth and development that could not be contemplated while all the participants were part-time volunteers with many other college commitments. At the same time it was very import-ant to maintain a creative and managerial role for students in accordance with the original educational concept that led to the development of the arts centre and the videotext service. This has happened naturally with the Central Studio, for its first use has been for a regular programme of student productions which generate an impetus and enthusiasm that unite performers, writers/composers, technicians, artists/designers, and provide a range of marketing, administrative and managerial tasks that can be shared with the permanent staff. A major challenge has been to maintain a sense of student commitment to the arts centre's professional programme, not merely as members of the audience and front-of-house helpers but through direct involvement in workshops, seminars, masterclasses and productions by professional actors and musicians. Several joint ventures have involved professional directors and playwrights working with student improvisations to create productions with mixed casts of professional actors and drama students.

By giving each year's course a specific development project as its focal point, Grapevine has sought to maintain something of the excitement and exhilaration experienced by the students who set up the videotext service. Thus, whilst students are constantly involved in the day-to-day maintenance of the service, researching and verifying information and revising the programme, they also have a new initiative to launch each year. This may be the negotiation and installation of new terminals, the introduction of a major new section of the programme, a fund-raising initiative to finance new developments, or a market research project leading to a complete revision and relaunch of the service. In this way the creative and developmental aspects have been preserved for successive groups of students.

One of the opportunities offered by the Queen Mary's main study programme was for students to work as a team. The ability to function effectively in cooperation with other people is one of the most common demands of adult life, yet few young people receive any preparation for this situation from their post-16 courses. There is occasional scope for teamwork on some vocational courses, but the academic curriculum places the emphasis unequivocally on individual achievement and competition, not on cooperative styles of working.

Cooperative groupwork

A significant attempt to remedy this omission is the joint North West TVEI/Liverpool University experiential groupwork project. This initiative, begun in 1987, promotes a partnership between education and industry in which student projects are devised by schools and colleges working with industry and Liverpool University. Students are introduced, through a series of minor projects, to the processes of experiential groupwork and then, in teams of four to five members, they undertake a major project negotiated with local industry. Each project aims to deliver a variety of transferable skills with the emphasis on learning how to work as a member of a team. Initially the projects were on integrated science topics, but options in modern

languages and other subjects have now been developed and there
are a number of interdisciplinary projects. The initiative has
been warmly welcomed by industry and by schools and colleges.
By 1992 there were 74 centres participating in the north-west, and
a national pilot scheme had been launched drawing in institutions from as far afield as Plymouth and the Isle of Wight.

From the outset the project leaders of the Liverpool initiative
have ensured that the students' work is closely monitored and
vigorously assessed, by both representatives of schools/colleges
and the firms involved. Assessment is by group log book, group
report and group presentation; there is also an element of peer
and self-assessment and an individual oral test. Liverpool
University awards a *Record of Achievement in Group Project
Work* certificate for each project completed.

In 1989 the Liverpool project leaders sought to bring their
initiative within the national system of academic qualifications
by submitting the experiential group project, through the Joint
Matriculation Board, to SEAC for acceptance as an AS level. The
council was impressed by the quality of the work being undertaken, but it could find no means, within existing assessment
procedures and constraints, of incorporating the project within
the A/AS system. It was therefore rejected.

This situation illustrates the inflexibility of the traditional A
level approach, with its narrow focus on subject-specific content
and terminal written assessment. Part of the rationale behind the
introduction of AS levels had been the possibility of exploring
new approaches to academic work, but without flexibility over
assessment that aim is impossible to realise. Not surprisingly,
therefore, the majority of AS syllabuses are simply imitations of
existing A levels and have done little to vary or enhance students'
learning experience.

Recommended curricular reforms in Scotland

The teaching and learning experience is strongly influenced by
syllabus design and methods of assessment, a fact refreshingly
recognised by the 1992 Howie Report on 14–18 education in
Scotland. The Howie Committee, set up in 1990 to review the
fifth and sixth years of Scottish secondary education,
recommends that the present Certificate of Education should be
replaced by a new three-year Scottish Baccalaureate. The

SCOTBAC would be designed to 'promote the development of a particular kind of course ethos' and to 'encourage students to take responsibility for their own learning'. The new courses would provide scope for cross-course assignments and for improved planning of schedules of homework and projects. The proposals

> offer greater opportunities for intensive study and individualised approaches to learning, including independent study and extended assignments. In particular, there will be a need to develop open and flexible learning. Educational technology – the evaluation of learning and teaching strategies with particular emphasis on the use of new media, methods and materials – must play a significant role.
>
> (Scottish Office Education Department, 1992)

Reforms based on broadening academic students' learning experience have a better starting point north of the border since the Scots already acknowledge the importance of students' continuing with a broad range of subjects beyond the statutory school-leaving age. Scottish Highers (the Higher Grade of the Scottish Certificate of Education) provide a Higginson-style programme that enables accomplished students to take four, five or even more subjects. They are, however, examined at 17 and the pressures entailed in reaching university entrance standard in one year are too much for many students: less than 10 per cent of the age group actually achieves five or more subjects. There are also concerns over the use made of Year 13 when students are given an odd mixture of options, including more Highers, more O grade courses (equivalent to GCSE) and a special Certificate of Sixth Year Studies. The Howie Committee has addressed problems of this kind whilst building on the accepted strengths of the broadly-based Higher School Certificate system.

Chapter 7

Student freedom and responsibility

INDEPENDENT STUDY

Adulthood, in the eyes of many teenagers, begins at 16. The transition from statutory school attendance to employment or voluntary education marks a change of situation and status no less significant than that associated with the legal age of majority two years later.

Whilst not necessarily sharing the views of their offspring and charges on the point at which childhood gives way to adulthood, most parents and teachers recognise that their relationship with older teenagers will benefit from less peremptory exercising of authority and more discussion and negotiation. Teachers, perhaps more than parents, see the 16–19 stage as one in which teenagers can accept a major share of responsibility for their own learning and personal development.

For generations of students this shift of emphasis has manifested itself mainly in an increased emphasis on independent study and greater freedom to manage their own work schedules. An allocation of 'free periods' during the working day has reduced staff contact time and ostensibly created space for background reading of the student's own choosing. In reality, though, students' private study and homework time have been spent largely in completing staff-directed assignments that have been selected as part of a systematic preparation for the final course examination. Few students have had the time or self-motivation to engage in substantial study of their own choice.

More imaginative syllabuses and methods of course delivery are changing this situation. An increasing number of students are now able to negotiate the topics and projects they undertake for assessed coursework – practical assignments, extended essays, case studies, work placements. Modular approaches have the potential to extend these decision-making responsibilities, enabling students to construct whole courses based on their particular interests and career aspirations.

Ultimately the aim of any education system must be the self-motivation of students. Records of achievement and action plans have involved both academic and vocational students more fully in programming their own work schedules and monitoring their own progress. Records of achievement develop skills of self-assessment as well as a heightened awareness of the impression students make on those who teach them. They have, too, an important formative role, indicating the action students need to take to capitalise on their strengths and to overcome weaknesses.

Compacts are a strategy to motivate students by encouraging realistic target setting and systematic work patterns. There are numerous *ad hoc* arrangements between the 16–19 sector and HE institutions, whereby the latter offer places to students on the basis of a wider range of evidence than the normal A level results. The students, in return, commit themselves to achieving a number of agreed goals. Although it lacks national coherence, the compact movement has appealed to both HE and schools/colleges as a means of encouraging disadvantaged students to aspire to and achieve a university or polytechnic place. There are similar arrangements between schools/colleges and employers, although the national shortage of jobs has tended to undermine this aspect of the compact movement.

DEGREES OF INDEPENDENCE

The trend towards greater student autonomy and responsibility has significant implications for the way in which an educational community functions. Once a school or college recognises the transitional state of the 16–19 age group – nicely balanced between childhood and adulthood, dependence and independence – it inevitably becomes engaged in a perennial debate on the extent to which responsibility should shift from staff to students – both within and outside the classroom.

Students' non-staff-contact-time illustrates the kind of issues that arise. Is this free time, or unequivocally private study time?

If the latter, how formally and rigidly is the ruling enforced? Does one allocate specific private study rooms, require students to attend, take a register, insist on individual study in silence? Or should students be able to choose the specific facilities that they require and be trusted to work unsupervised in studios, laboratory prep rooms, workshops and libraries?

What exactly constitutes 'private study'? Does it extend to reading a newspaper, discussing a TV documentary with a friend, improvising on the piano? If non-staff-contact-time is 'free time', how free is 'free'? May students have a workout in the gym, make a phone call, play pool in the common room, take an early lunch in the refectory? Are they free to leave the site when they please? If students have a block of free time, may they turn up at school or college at mid-day or leave after lunch? In short, if students are responsible for meeting their work deadlines, should they not decide precisely how they organise their time to fulfil these obligations? And, if they are mature enough to take responsibility for their work, should they not have the same autonomy with regard to their lifestyle in general?

These are crucial questions for institutions catering for the 16–19 age group in its transition from dependence to independence. Schools and colleges recognise that the age of 16 is a watershed at which young people must begin to take control of their own destiny and be exposed to adult responsibilities and decisions. The question is how far to go in releasing controls and relaxing supervision: the exact balance between dependence and independence is important. Specific changes of emphasis can have a significant effect on staff/student relationships. Mistakes are difficult to rectify: once relinquished, controls are not so easily reimposed.

In any 16–19 community there are various levels of maturity: every measure taken in recognition of the general readiness of students to exercise more responsibility will leave some individuals vulnerable. The further one moves in the direction of student autonomy, the stronger one's guidance and care systems need to be to support those who experience difficulty in handling the responsibilities and freedoms offered them.

Each institution takes its own decisions on these matters in accordance with its particular educational philosophy. Whole staff policies towards students of 16–19 are somewhat easier to implement in colleges dealing solely with this age group. Most institutions have to consider the needs of a wider age range. In FE and tertiary colleges, 16–19 students are the junior members of the community; in schools they are, of course, the most senior. This difference inevitably influences staff attitudes.

COLLEGE LIFESTYLES

In FE and tertiary colleges the presence of a large number of mature students sets the pattern of student freedom and responsibility and leads to the expectation that the 16–19 age group will conform to adult patterns of behaviour. There is an underlying assumption that students will exercise self-discipline in meeting their course requirements and set reasonable standards of self-control, decency and consideration to others in their day-to-day relationships. There are few regulations and formalities and no regimentation over such matters as appearance and demeanour. General behaviour is regulated largely by consensus, so that smoking, for example, is confined to agreed areas. Excesses are curbed at the discretion of individual members of staff, or even students, rather than by a coordinated enforcement of a published list of rules.

The extent to which their sons and daughters are treated as adults in FE and tertiary colleges can come as rather a shock to parents, and not just to the staid and reactionary:

> I remember, when college letters were sent to my daughters, thinking: 'Hey, just a minute, how about writing to me? I'm only the bloody father after all'. Nor have I ever felt entirely relaxed at the freedom to wander into town when not in lectures. Why should my kids skive off into town? Damn it, at their age I was busy skiving in the school library, chatting to my mates instead of revising.
>
> (Ted Wragg, 1991)

Colleges recognise the problem for parents, but are generally reluctant to enter into the sort of relationship with them that is developed in schools and maintained in the sixth form. Ted Wragg quotes John Capey, Principal of Exeter Tertiary College, on the subject:

> 'At 16, we'll communicate a bit more with parents, but at 17 or 18 they have to be given responsibility.'

There is a real dilemma here that is rather more serious than Ted Wragg's typically tongue-in-cheek comments imply. Whatever adjustments one makes to *in loco parentis* responsibilities in recognition of older teenagers' developing maturity, the legal age of adulthood remains 18. With students below that age, parents have a right to be consulted on major decisions affecting their sons and daughters and kept informed of any problems that may arise.

Just as the image of university undergraduate freedom is often a greater reality for arts students than for those following science courses, there are considerable differences of lifestyle in an FE or tertiary college according to the courses that students follow. Those on specialist vocational courses can lead a very structured existence, with considerably more staff contact hours than A level students experience. The work ethic exerts a strong influence on these students. Thus regular attendance and punctuality, a good presence and smart appearance, basic courtesies and good manners will all be stressed as qualities that enhance employment prospects – for mature as well as younger students.

Particular departments may establish their own codes of conduct and practice appropriate to the specific careers for which they train students and the institutions that offer them work experience. Vocational students often function in a closely-knit group which has its own culture, reflecting that of a particular profession or working environment. The personal competences that vocational departments seek to develop are obviously more specific and work-related than the general character training which is the concern of schools. Nevertheless, departments can play an important part in students' personal development and influence their general response to college.

There are fewer variations of student lifestyle in sixth form colleges. Although entitled for many years to enrol adults, sixth form colleges have concentrated almost exclusively on the 16–19 age group and the great majority of their students have followed academic programmes. Vocational work has tended to be of a general or pre-vocational nature, rather than occupation-specific. There has been a clear recognition of the need for strong care systems and close links with the home. The regular evening meeting when parents do the rounds of all their sons' and daughters' teachers is one of the ways in which sixth form colleges reflect the school tradition to which they have always belonged.

In their early years, sixth form colleges tended to be more protective towards their students than they are now. As they have developed, the colleges have placed greater trust in their students, relaxing their registration requirements and offsite rules, their procedures for reporting absence and lateness, and their arrangements for private study. Distinctions between lower and upper sixth have disappeared. Common room and refectory facilities have been greatly improved. Sixth form colleges have created their own particular style of managing the 16–19 age group, settling for a compromise of freedom within clearly marked boundaries. There is an element of negotiation which allows for some flexibility over the treatment of individuals according to circumstances. The result is a community that is less paternalistic and 'safe' than a school, but which exercises closer supervision and support than an FE college.

Such generalisations have immediately to be qualified. Considerable differences exist between institutions within the separate school and FE traditions. Conversely there are marked similarities between some sixth form and tertiary colleges. The difference between the number of full- and part-time students and between the size of the 16–19 age group and that of the mature student enrolment helps to determine the character of a tertiary college.

Overall size, too, has a major influence on the extent of student freedom and responsibility. For example, as sixth form college numbers have increased, decisions to allow students to study at home when they have no classes have sometimes had more to do with pressure on accommodation than eagerness to place greater trust in students. Expediency exerts a particular influence on the degree of student autonomy in very large FE and tertiary colleges, where formalised systems of supervision and control are often impractical because of the multiplicity of functions and sites.

THE SIXTH FORM WITHIN THE SCHOOL CULTURE

Sixth form lifestyles have undergone great changes in recent years as schools have responded to the need to release their older students from much of the staff direction and supervision that apply to younger pupils. Many sixth forms have now acquired collegiate-style accommodation and facilities and offer their senior students responsibilities and freedoms similar to those enjoyed by their contemporaries at college. Without these developments, some comprehensive schools would have had great difficulty in retaining their sixth forms in competition with neighbouring post-16 institutions. Selective schools too have improved their sixth form facilities, but are more likely to expect their senior students to conform to much the same routines and rules as the rest of the school. Concessions to sixth form students' approaching adulthood are not required as an inducement to remain at school where staying on at 16 is the norm and A level success is virtually guaranteed.

The forward-looking comprehensive school seeks to provide its sixth form students with the best of the school and college worlds. College-style amenities, relationships and freedoms are combined with a familial environment in which it is hoped students will experience a strong sense of belonging and receive support from staff who know them really well. How attractive this blend is to students may depend to some extent on their pre-16 experience. Those who have been successful and enjoyed the trust and support of staff will probably be happy to remain within the community they know and like. Others will be ready for a change, particularly if they suspect that a legacy of earlier immaturity might affect their chances of being treated as adults in the sixth form.

The ability of a comprehensive school to maintain a viable sixth form is affected by its location. Rural teenagers are inclined to be less impatient with a familial-style community than their more sophisticated urban counterparts, particularly if the college alternative entails a long daily journey. In urban areas students have more options at 16 and are better informed about them. Although this generally works to the disadvantage of schools, some enter into schemes of joint provision with nearby FE institutions, thereby retaining their sixth form students, but extending their course options by releasing them to the college for some components of their programme.

Schools are involved in a difficult balancing act with their sixth form students. On the one hand, they need to free them from regulations and routines designed for younger pupils. On the other, a major argument for retaining post-16 students in schools is the beneficial influence they exert on the community and its culture: they become role models who set an example of commitment to the institution and of conformity to its code of conduct.

The lifestyle of the sixth form sets it apart from the rest of the school. Staff are less directive and formal in their general dealings with members of the sixth form and rarely use the sanctions they apply to the rest of the school. Students are given considerable discretion over study routines, use of facilities and how they dress. At the same time, there are usually clear expectations that sixth form students will recognise and accept the importance of adhering to the value system and standards of behaviour that constitute a school's distinctive character and culture.

Moreover, it is generally expected that they will devote some of their time to serving the school, assuming prefectorial responsibilities, helping in the library, and sometimes assisting teachers in the classroom with less able children. They also help organise and run extra-curricular activities, captaining teams and taking on the role of secretary to clubs and societies. These arrangements are regarded not merely as a one-way process in which students give something back to the institution from which they have received their secondary education, but also as a means of providing senior members of the community with valuable management and leadership experience.

This function is most explicit in the independent sector. The boys' public school, in particular, has, as a central objective, the preparation of an elite for leadership roles in society. The exercising of authority by senior boys is a significant part of this process. Traditionally, prefects in public schools wielded as much power outside the classroom as the masters did within it. They administered corporal punishment until the second half of this century and the notorious fagging system – younger boys acting as servants to seniors – persisted very much longer. Although the extreme forms of prefectorial authority have now been curbed, sixth form leadership roles remain extremely important and they are usually taken very seriously by those to whom they are entrusted. Most of the responsibilities fall to boys in their final year, but they can involve the lower sixth, particularly in boarding schools, where well-developed house systems extend the leadership opportunities.

Prefectorial duties and the tasks involved in being a club

captain or secretary of a society may be quite time-consuming. In the maintained day school, students are inclined to weigh the value of the experience, and the extent to which it enhances their curriculum vitae, against the loss of study time or the effect on their social life or part-time job. Some are reluctant to take on such extra commitments. In the public boarding school such considerations do not arise, even though the duties may be considerably more onerous: leadership roles are a natural culmination of the pupils' development and carry much social status and prestige.

In the most famous public schools the sixth form – itself an elite within an elite – has its own sub-divisions and hierarchies. At Eton, for example, the school's prefectorial body, Eton Society or 'Pop', is an especially privileged and exclusive group. Consisting of twenty boys, it has many features of a gentlemen's club with a largely self-selected membership, outgoing prefects choosing their successors. This system of patronage and exclusive membership extends to some of the higher status extra-curricular activities, such as the wine-tasting society. Eton has over a hundred club and society officers, the more prestigious of them bearing grand titles such as Keeper of Fives, Captain of the Boats, Master of the Beagles, and Pipe Major. Forty extra-curricular responsibilities qualify for the special status of School Officer, which entitles the holder to wear 'stick-ups' (wing-collars).

Girls' independent schools are less traditionalist than their male counterparts. The public schools, in particular, are keenly aware of the need to prepare girls for their modern roles in society, not those that applied in the past. It is still possible to find the finishing-school approach, with young ladies learning a range of respectable pastimes and accomplishments to occupy their leisure hours as genteel wives and mothers. In the modern public school, however, young women are taught to develop their minds and individuality and to compete with men.

The trend for boys' public schools to admit girls, particularly to their sixth forms, has increased the emphasis that the girls' schools place on the benefits of single sex education, especially the importance of girls being in an environment where leadership role models are women. Independent girls' schools have also moved further than the boys' public schools towards creating an adult atmosphere in the sixth form, often dispensing with uniform and other forms of regimentation. If it wishes to retain its sixth form, the girls' independent school must avoid, at all costs, the convent image of detachment from the real world.

Sixth form students' experience, like that of younger pupils, differs greatly, according to the nature of the school and its clientele. Nevertheless, by virtue of their membership of a community consisting mainly of younger teenagers, all sixth form students have dimensions to their lifestyle that do not exist in a post-16 college. Their responsibilities are not only to themselves but to their school community and the children in it.

College students do not, of course, work in isolation from their fellows and without consideration for other people. Like adults, they develop allegiances and commitments – to vocational departments, particular academic courses, teams, drama groups, orchestras and many other units within their college. They often give their time unstintingly to the organisation of their own social occasions and fund-raising activities, to social service and charity events. They are not, however, inbred with a sense of belonging to the whole institution or with a duty to behave in certain ways to set an example to younger children or to create a favourable image in public. They do not sing school songs or attend daily assemblies. They have no need to put out cigarettes or conceal half-eaten apples if about to pass a member of staff in the street.

Who gains and loses in these different situations is a matter of opinion. Students are more in tune with the college environment, but our society is slow to relinquish the past and has yet to make up its mind where the 16–19 age group truly belongs. This ambivalence is illustrated by some of the anomalies of the 1992 Further and Higher Education Act. For example, the Act clearly categorises members of the 16–19 age group who remain at school as *pupils*, not *students*. Again, having removed all other distinctions between sixth form and FE colleges, it stipulates that those corporate colleges that were previously run under schools regulations must make provision at least once a week for an act of Christian worship and include in their curricula a course of religious education. Colleges that were previously run under FE regulations are not required to make such provision.

Chapter 8

Managing the curriculum

THE DEPARTMENT

There are three key management functions in an educational establishment: the delivery of the curriculum, the care and welfare of students, and the supporting administrative services and procedures. The trend in institutions of the size and complexity of those catering for the 16–19 age group is to establish separate structures and related senior staff roles to facilitate these three functions.

The main management unit for delivering the 16–19 curriculum is the department, a group of staff responsible for the courses in a specific academic subject or vocational area. This unit is a natural expression and consequence of the compartmentalised approach to education and training and, at the same time, a strong factor in maintaining that tradition. In focusing their teaching on a particular specialism, staff identify with a group which has a shared enthusiasm and knowledge base and which provides them with both security and support. At its best, the department offers its members a dynamic context for deepening their scholarship and increasing their expertise. The wellbeing of their specialism becomes a common cause, manifest not least in the effort to recruit 16+ students onto the department's courses and to provide a new generation of specialists.

Whilst the members of a department identify strongly with a particular academic subject or vocational area, they are by no means always united in their approach to their courses or in the way in which they deliver them. Teachers work in an independent and self-regulated way, separated most of the time from their colleagues, responding intuitively to the fluctuating moods of their own classes, constantly assessing and refining what works for them in their particular circumstances. They develop an individual style and an allegiance to particular approaches, methods and resources. Staff in the latter stages of their career can be particularly difficult to persuade that it would be beneficial to change ways of working that have served them well for many years.

Faced with strongly-held beliefs in different educational methods, it is tempting for heads of departments to busy themselves improving administrative routines, in preference to tackling the key issues of syllabus choice, course design, teaching method and quality control. Progress comes either where there is a natural consensus over the way in which the quality of the students' learning experience can be improved or where a determined head of department works patiently and diplomatically through like-minded colleagues to persuade sceptics and facilitate change. Reform by diktat simply drives tensions and conflicts beneath the surface: staff have to be convinced that what they are doing is right to make it work.

In the most academic schools, where the system of subject departments has found its strongest expression, every specialism has tended to aspire to the status of a department. Heads of department thus range from part-time members of staff struggling to keep a minority subject alive to someone in charge of the whole of the English or mathematics teaching. The larger departments may have staff designated or recognised as no. 2 and no. 3 in the hierarchy, with greater responsibilities and higher salaries than those in charge of minority subjects. In this situation, heads of department meetings create an illogical division of managers and managed. They are also often too large and unwieldy to fulfil an executive function.

Until the 1970s there was, in fact, little effective middle-management in schools. This was of no great consequence when the only important decisions concerning the curriculum were those connected with individual teachers' course design, lesson preparation and classroom organisation. In those days, which some teachers recall with a certain nostalgia, the principal tasks for the head of department were to spend a small annual allowance on books and equipment and to keep an eye on the occasional probationary teacher. However, in the 1970s and 1980s a growth of interest in concepts of curriculum evaluation, development and management led many comprehensive schools to establish more effective structures for curricular policy-making, implementation and quality control. Numerous Schools Council initiatives played a decisive part in these developments.

THE FACULTY SYSTEM

A popular response to the need for more effective management structures to deliver the curriculum was the faculty system. Staff were divided into a small number of roughly equal-sized groups which linked teachers with similar curricular interests. Subject specialists were encouraged to become less insular by exploring the common ground within, for example, the social sciences, creative arts or science, design and technology. Heads of faculty then emerged as a tier of upper-middle management who, chaired by headteacher or deputy, could take a shared responsibility for the direction of the whole curriculum.

As an administrative and consultative unit the faculty is a convenient and manageable division of staff, sufficiently flexible to be adapted to differences and fluctuations in the size of institutions. In terms of managing the curriculum, however, it requires members of staff - and particularly those who constitute the management team - to think and act on behalf of the faculty, not to defend a particular subject interest. Where a strong departmental identity is retained within a faculty it is often difficult to establish a faculty policy over such matters as course design and teaching methods and thus to achieve a sense of coherence and common purpose.

In the 11-18 comprehensive, faculty staff teach different age groups and levels of work, as well as different subjects. For example, the needs of the 16-19 age group are a recurring issue for some staff, but of no more than general interest to those without a sixth form teaching commitment. Faculty heads sometimes hold separate meetings for their sixth form staff. More frequently there is a forum that cuts across the faculty structure and brings all the school's sixth form teachers together, perhaps under the leadership of a deputy head or director of sixth form studies.

Whatever strategy is employed for consideration of the sixth form curriculum, some sensitivity is required over the priority and agenda time given to this aspect of a school's work. Sixth form staff can appear a privileged group. The A level teaching, in particular, is much sought after, for it enhances both job satisfaction and career prospects, and often brings with it additional salary. Those who have no part in this prestigious and attractive work can be resentful if a school appears to overstress its importance.

With the advent of the National Curriculum, management priorities in schools have in fact tended to swing to lower- and middle-school work. Whilst aware of the major changes that lie ahead for the sixth form, staff have understandably concentrated on the immediate task of meeting the new curricular requirements for years 7-11. The changes for younger pupils are now specified; those affecting the sixth form remain, at national level, undefined and uncertain. Teachers can hardly be blamed for waiting for the fog to clear and perhaps leaving most of the initiatives, insofar as they lie with the teaching profession, to their colleagues in the colleges.

In sixth form colleges concentration on the 16-19 age group gives greater coherence to the departmental unit, although there are still variations in the level and status of work. The importance of specialist A level work also strengthens departments. At the same time, the range of subjects offered and the great variation in the number of students studying them makes the identification of every specialism as a department even more problematic than in a school. Of the many school features that sixth form colleges retained, the system of separate subject departments was probably the least appropriate.

The case for faculties has certainly been a strong one in the colleges because of the particularly fragmented management structure and uneven groupings of staff created by the departmental system. Attempts to combine traditional departments within a new faculty structure have, however, encountered some difficulties. The variation in size of departments is one of them: some departments consist of one or two people; others are almost large enough to function as management units on their own. There are inevitably tensions if such very different sized departments retain their separate identity as management units within a larger team. Heads of large departments can feel their status doubly diminished: first, by a structure that appears to equate them with colleagues whose responsibilities may be less than members of their own department and, second, by themselves having to report to a faculty head whose coordinating role may seem no more important than their own. This feeling is likely to be strengthened among heads of departments who previously had a management role in a school situation where they reported directly to the headteacher or a deputy.

In such situations the full faculty meeting chaired by its head can be a difficult occasion. The function of such meetings is of course to air matters of general concern and to encourage staff to identify with the faculty, as opposed to the departmental unit. Considerable restraint and sensitivity are required of both faculty and departmental heads if the two allegiances are to be seen as complementary and not in competition. Once territorial struggles start to dominate discussion, meetings become counterproductive.

Some faculty heads try to avoid such difficulties by sharing their coordinating function with heads of major departments, for example by rotating the chairing of meetings. Others protect their heads of departments' management role by dispensing with full faculty meetings, or confining them to occasional seminars on general educational topics rather than specific management issues. They then seek to fulfil their own management function by working through heads of department, either separately or as a group. Heads of department meetings are likely to be most successful when departments are of comparable size and their managers of equal status and on the same salary.

A major weakness of the faculty system in schools and sixth form colleges is that it has little rationale for students, most of whom have programmes of study drawn from different disciplines and therefore no strong sense of belonging to any one faculty. Thus the concept of curricular integration, which is the ideological basis for the way in which departments are grouped in a faculty system, has no practical outlet or means of expression in course terms. It is usually regarded as impracticable to run integrated programmes of work for the minority of students who do operate solely within a faculty, as they are taught in classes where the majority of students study cross-faculty subject combinations. This militates against involving students in any detailed exploration of the concepts and processes that unite the subjects within the faculty.

FE CURRICULUM MANAGEMENT

The management of the curriculum in FE colleges is on a much larger scale than that of schools and most sixth form colleges. The terminology and attitudes are also different. First, and most importantly, a 'department' in an FE college is traditionally the term used for a division of staff responsible for all the courses in a broad vocational area, what in fact a school thinks of as a faculty. If one includes its part-time staff, a large FE department may consist of more lecturers than the total staff of an 11-18 school. The number of departments varies with the size of the institution and the range of its work, but four to six staff divisions are usually regarded as the norm.

With the steady growth in the size of colleges and increased diversification of their courses, there has been a tendency for departments to sub-divide into subject sections or course/teaching teams. The essential difference between this situation and that of the school system is that the movements have been in opposite directions. The smaller units in the FE system have been formed within an established division, whereas in schools and sixth form colleges faculties have been created by grouping together existing single-subject departments.

The FE department is normally a much more autonomous and insular unit than a faculty in a school or sixth form college. The head of department has acquired delegated responsibilities from the principal that go well beyond delivery of the curriculum. Together, heads of department constitute a formidable senior management team led by the principal in the role of *general manager*. A significant factor in the FE department's insularity and autonomy has been the more or less complete responsibility it has had for a division of the college's students. Vocational students are admitted to a specific department and normally follow a package course, taught, monitored and assessed by staff from that department. Even students' general education, once the responsibility of a separate general studies department, has now been integrated into their main course and therefore becomes the responsibility of the same team of staff.

On the other hand, diversification of courses for the 16-19 age

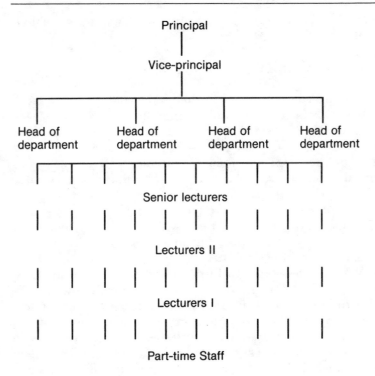

Figure 8.1 Traditional FE management structure

group has led to the formation of a number of course teams that cut across the traditional departmental system. This occurred with many of the earlier Youth Training schemes, the CPVE and also with provision for students with special needs. The growth in the number of GCE and GCSE students, many of whom follow cross-curricular programmes of study, has also had a significant effect on the way in which some FE colleges are organised. Tertiary colleges, in particular, have introduced various forms of academic division, including matrix systems of management with a college approach to admissions and time-tabling. Heads of department become *directors* with college-wide management roles, or *deans of study* overseeing very broad groupings of allied subjects from which they assemble students' programmes of study in consultation with specialist teams of staff led by *heads of subject schools, course teams, divisions* or *sections.*

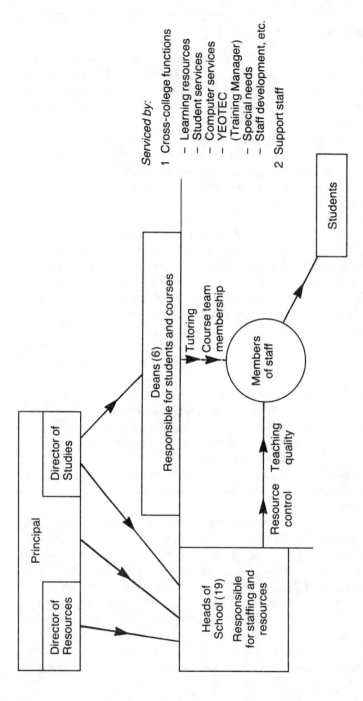

Figure 8.2 Yeovil Tertiary College management structure, 1992

THE FLEXIBLE COLLEGE

The drive for increased access and participation has introduced the concept of the flexible college, able to compile programmes of study to meet very different individual needs, instead of pigeon-holing students into pre-arranged courses. Learner-centred programmes of study challenge traditional assumptions about academic subject specialisms and coherent vocational courses and, if the current trend towards modularity and progressive systems of credit accumulation continues, curriculum management will take on a very different meaning. Current divisions between departments, subjects and vocational areas will become more fluid as new staff teams form and re-form to design and deliver courses and programmes of study drawn from across the curriculum. These new teams will be unified, not by staff specialisms, but by a common purpose in providing a set of learning experiences that has value and relevance to a particular group or category of student at a given point in time. Leadership roles will relate to specific tasks, some of them short-term, and be spread round more staff.

Departments will, of course, continue to have a very important role. Modules will rely heavily on specialists for their design and delivery. Many students will continue to follow a closely integrated programme, or at least one that includes a core of studies from a single subject or vocational area. Even those who seek more varied and individualised programmes of study will often rely on specialists for guidance on progression routes through the modular curriculum. Departmental staff will, however, also have other roles, liaising across departments over joint courses and being members of cross-curricular course design and teaching teams.

The ultimate learner-centred curriculum will provide every student with an individually appropriate programme of study made up of a variety of learning experiences: classes, seminars, workshops, tutorials, group projects, work experience and self-learning units. Staff timetables will match this variety, involving a mixture of class and small group teaching, workshop management, project supervision and responsibilities for designing courses, modules and learning materials. As *learning managers*, staff will have a number of students to advise on their programmes of study, assessing needs, agreeing individual targets, providing appropriate learning opportunities, monitoring and reviewing programmes, assessing achievement. In this role, teachers and lecturers will need to be capable of generalist as well as specialist perspectives, tutoring students on cross-curricular programmes as well as those working mainly in one subject area.

THE MANAGEMENT OF RESOURCES

These developments are already having an impact, not only on the deployment of staff, but on the management of other resources: materials and equipment, furniture and accommodation. Faculties and departments have always sought proprietorship of their own resources. They have been most successful in this respect where the rooms, facilities and equipment they require are demonstrably specialist and unsuitable for general use. Thus FE departments, with their heavy investment in plant and equipment associated with specific occupations, have functioned very much as self-contained units, having complete control of their accommodation and equipment and building up their own resource banks of information and teaching materials. In schools, science and creative studies faculties incline towards this situation, although timetabling of classes and rooming arrangements are usually not within their direct control.

A number of factors have contributed to a move towards more central control of resources in both schools and colleges. The education service, not unlike the health service, has been finding it increasingly difficult in the last 10–15 years to obtain the resources that it seeks: politicians point to a steady increase in funding; educationists argue that the cost of equipment, books and other materials rises more steeply than the delegated budget allocations. The real problem, however, is that the aspirations of the education and health services, and society's expectations of them, have outrun government determination and ability to foot the bill.

We no longer feel that it is acceptable for students to share out-of-date textbooks or to learn a trade on obsolete machinery. Yet the speed of change means that books and machinery constantly have to be renewed to keep abreast of curricular developments and modern employment practices. New academic syllabuses, with their greater emphasis on current issues, practical projects and varied assessment procedures, make heavier demands on resources. Changes in employment patterns have required FE colleges to establish whole new areas of operation, some of them – like business studies – very costly in terms of hardware. Much of the equipment and materials previously associated with a specific part of the curriculum are now considered appropriate, or indeed necessary, by other subject areas. Resource banks of current printed materials have a much wider use than specialist textbooks. Computers, in particular, have applications right across the curriculum.

All these factors have compelled schools and colleges to seek ways of optimising their use of resources. Most have concluded that this means more centralised provision. Libraries have incorporated resource banks, databases, tape and CD collections and playback facilities, and been extended to provide resource-based learning centres and information technology workshop areas. Staff resource centres provide a range of reprographic/desktop publishing facilities and audio-visual aids, and some-times photographic/TV equipment and TV and radio recording services. The role of clerical and technical staff in libraries and resource centres is changing as they become more involved in the preparation and use of learning materials and self-study pro-grammes.

Even traditional FE departments are having to relinquish some of their self-sufficiency and autonomy in favour of college-wide systems of administration and resource-management. A typical matrix structure has two branches: one comprising departments (in the faculty sense) with responsibility for courses, students, timetabling and deployment of staff; the other combin-ing a number of administrative groupings, often called *schools*, which are responsible for the utilisation of resources such as equipment, the allocation of rooms, and the deployment of technicians. On a smaller scale, teams of academic and ancillary staff, with their own director, are being developed in schools and sixth form colleges to manage resources. In some instances all the institution's administrative services and resources are brought together under the management of a deputy head or vice-principal.

As well as being a more economic way of resourcing a school or college, a central system of provision has greater flexibility, being able to respond to the needs of cross-curricular staff teams as well as to departments. It increases horizontal communication and liaison, balancing the vertical and hierarchical pattern of departmental relationships. Such two-way systems will become increasingly important as more students study across the curriculum and the academic/vocational divide.

The private study component of students' programmes of study has obvious accommodation implications. At the most basic level, the pressure on library space creates a need for additional reading/writing rooms. With increasing recognition of the range of activities appropriate to independent study, requirements have diversified and become much more demanding. Few institutions, however, can look forward to the acquisition of purpose-built, multi-resource sites. The best that can be achieved is likely to be the modification and re-equipping of existing rooms. Ideally, large flexible spaces are required with adjustable partitioning and direct access to tutorial rooms and storage. Ironically, some of the institutions least well-endowed with rooms suitable for conversion to resource areas are those with relatively new buildings. Mistaken assumptions about group size led to frequent overprovision of small set rooms in sixth form college buildings and sixth form teaching blocks during the 1970s and 1980s.

This situation reflects the need for educationists – particularly teachers – to be closely involved in the design of new teaching accommodation and conversion projects. Too frequently such involvement is limited, confined to the early planning stages and not maintained throughout the development of a building or extensive conversion programme. The lengthy gap in time between the initial planning and completion of such projects means that early agreements and specifications become lost in a mass of practical problems, or modified because of unforeseen financial constraints. Architects and large building-firms are prone to switching personnel from one job to another with a consequent breakdown in communication. With the declining LEA role in education, it is particularly important that building and conversion projects are continually monitored by the institutions themselves.

The need for large flexible spaces is not confined to resource areas. The changes taking place in the way 16–19 courses are delivered require more access to practical facilities in the classroom. Space is needed for equipment and for students to work with materials such as maps, plans, spreadsheets, documents and reference books. Projection and display facilities should be available for all staff. Teaching spaces and furniture have to be adaptable to a range of learning situations. Staff should be able to distance one-to-one consultations and tutoring from a class working on its own or in groups.

Resources will always be too limited to provide such flexibility in every room and thus for every teacher simultaneously. The objective has to be for every major division of the curriculum to have a range of rooms that provide flexible teaching and tutorial facilities for every team of staff. In the meantime, central control of resources can help to ensure that departments or faculties that enjoy high-grade accommodation and facilities do not deny all access to other less fortunate subject areas.

Chapter 9

Student care and guidance

SIXTH FORM SYSTEMS

In the education of young children, teaching and care are inseparable, both being the responsibility of the class teacher. In the secondary school, pupils are taught by many different subject specialists but are in the care of one 'form teacher'. Forms consist of about 30 pupils, fewer in independent schools. They are grouped into larger divisions: usually horizontally in year groups, or sometimes vertically, in houses. The work of form teachers is coordinated by a year or house head. A deputy head is often in overall charge of the care system.

In the past, sixth forms conformed to whatever system applied to the rest of the school. In the year system there were separate lower and upper sixths and each year was sub-divided, often into science and arts A level divisions, and a separate form for the general or non-A level sixth, where it existed. Selective schools still favour the separation of lower and upper sixth and divisions within each year that group students according to subject background. The size of groups has, however, been reduced, with sixth form tutors having responsibility for fewer students than form teachers elsewhere in the school.

In a house system the head of house, or house master/mistress in the independent sector, is responsible for a division of pupils spanning the school's full age range and including sixth form students. The latter are key figures in the house hierarchy, assuming a variety of management responsibilities and leadership roles. Much of the contact between house staff and sixth form students concerns house affairs and the students' roles in relation to them. The house system is strongest in the schools in which it originated: the boys' public schools, where all pupils belong to one of several boarding houses. Some day schools have established effective care systems based on the house concept. More frequently, however, house divisions in a day school are simply a strategy for encouraging a sense of allegiance and commitment to the competing sides in organised competitions, particularly team games.

Comprehensive schools are less inclined than selective schools to encourage inter-house rivalry and to formalise differences between categories of student through their management structures. Thus comprehensive school sixth forms are often well-integrated, with everyone sharing the same accommodation and minimal distinctions drawn between years 12 and 13. Tutor groups are often completely mixed, containing students from both years and different subject/course backgrounds. Tutors thus oversee their students' progress and welfare throughout their time in the sixth form and obtain considerable help from year 13 students in advising year 12 on such issues as planning work routines, revising for exams, job and HE applications and interviews. Where tutor groups are drawn from one year, tutors often stay with their group throughout their time in the sixth form in order to maintain continuity of care and guidance. This strategy is, however, uneconomical on staffing if the departure of one-year students leaves tutor groups very depleted in year 13. Combining groups may be necessary in this situation.

All schools that retain a sixth form stress the benefits that young people derive from being part of a continuing system of care and guidance. The accumulated knowledge and understanding that the school has of its students are considered particularly valuable in the sixth form when tutors are helping students to meet the demands of independent learning and offering guidance on crucial decisions over career and higher education options.

SIXTH FORM COLLEGE SYSTEMS

Early opposition to the development of sixth form colleges often concentrated on the break in continuity of care and guidance caused by a change of institutions at 16. There were doubts whether colleges would ever be able to establish close relationships with students who only stayed for one year and whether they would do justice to two-year students when writing their references for higher education, after little more than one year's acquaintance.

The sixth form college response to this criticism was twofold. First, processes of admission and induction were established that enabled senior staff to work closely with contributory/partner schools in order to get to know each year's prospective college entrants long before their arrival. Second, almost all staff were given a clearly-defined personal tutoring role with responsibility for the progress and welfare of about 15/16 students. The admissions exercise and care system in sixth form colleges are closely linked, with the same senior staff managing them both. There are normally from three to six senior staff involved, either vice-principals, or senior tutors paid on or near the top of the salary scale. In some colleges vice-principals and senior tutors both lead teams of tutors; in others there is a line management with several senior tutors reporting to a vice-principal in overall charge.

This heavy investment of senior staff indicates the importance attached to the sixth form college care systems. In the early days of sixth form colleges more thought and effort were devoted to this aspect of college organisation and management than to the corresponding curricular structures, the latter being refined and

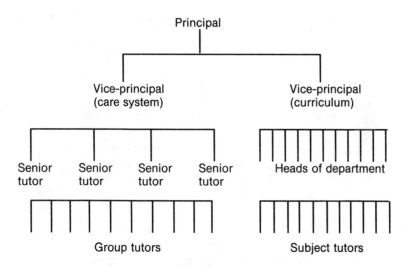

Figure 9.1 Early sixth form college management structure.

improved more gradually. The colleges were determined to overcome the alleged disadvantage of the break at 16, by ensuring that all students had a member of staff who would get to know them really well – both as a student and as a person.

Sixth form college tutors work in teams of six to a dozen or more, according to the size of the college and the number of team leaders. The vice-principals and/or senior tutors seek to maintain agreed policies, standard procedures and quality control. Team meetings often include an element of staff development as well as routine coordination and administration. Case studies may be used to stimulate discussion on such matters as confidentiality of information on students, referral procedures and recurrent personal and domestic problems.

In some colleges the students of a team of tutors are treated as a unit, meeting occasionally as a division, perhaps for careers/ higher education talks, a component of the college's personal development programme or an entertainment or social activity of some kind. In the majority of colleges, however, the tutor group is the single student unit in the care system. Colleges seek to keep

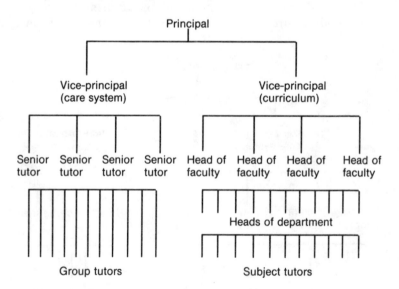

Figure 9.2 Sixth form college care system and curriculum management structure with faculties.

the size of tutor groups as small as possible and some reduce the norm of 15/16 to as few as 12, by involving senior managers as well as all other members of staff in the tutoring role.

The real test of an institution's commitment to the care and welfare of students is the extent to which tutors are made to feel that the work is of the utmost importance. There are some colleges that believe this is best achieved by minimising senior management functions and devolving full responsibility to tutors. In this situation the personal or group tutor's responsibility includes the interviewing and admission of students, reporting to and liaising with parents, and deciding on referrals to central student services. One vice-principal coordinates the tutors' work.

Problems of standardising procedures and maintaining equity of treatment are increased in this system and inexperienced tutors are unlikely to receive the level of support they would have from a senior tutor responsible for a small team of tutors. On the other hand, tutors are left in no doubt of the trust and confidence placed in them and there is potential for enhanced job satisfaction, personal growth and career advancement. At the other extreme, where school or college senior management expects to take all the important decisions concerning students, tutors may feel that they are simply go-betweens, conveying information, interpreting the institution's policies and procedures, dealing with routine administration – but not carrying much genuine responsibility for students' progress and wellbeing. Good management avoids this situation by flexible leadership, giving experienced and effective tutors maximum responsibility, but providing strong support for those who lack experience and/or confidence in the tutoring role.

THE ROLE OF THE TUTOR

There is a perennial debate in both school sixth forms and sixth form colleges as to whether tutors should teach all the members of their tutor group. The argument in favour of their doing so is that the best way to get to know students is to teach them. The counter view is that students' performance sometimes varies considerably from subject to subject and the component of their programme taught by their tutor might give a distorted view of their work as a whole. Moreover, some students appear more willing to talk openly about personal problems to tutors with whom they do not have a classroom relationship. There are also practical considerations: given the complexity of students' programmes of study and the great variety of their subject combinations, it is organisationally quite difficult to group them so that they are all taught for one of their main subjects by their tutor.

A large majority of sixth form colleges have decided on completely mixed tutor groups – different years, sexes, contributory/partner schools and college courses. Those that group students with a component of their study programme in common, thereby enabling their tutor to teach them, usually mix groups in all other ways. Only occasionally are years 12 and 13 separated or special arrangements made for one-year students and those staying for a third year.

Sixth form and sixth form college tutors see their groups daily, or twice daily, for registration, administration and communication purposes. They then have a weekly tutorial of about an hour, or several shorter periods of group time spread throughout the week. These sessions may be used for formal or informal groupwork, or in order to see individual students about their progress, career/higher education applications and general welfare. The balance between the group sessions and one-to-one counselling varies and is often left to the discretion of the tutor.

Many tutors work very hard to establish the social cohesion of their tutor group, organising or encouraging various group activities – outings, fund-raising and community service initiatives, social events, inter-group competitions and sports contests. A tutor group that gels through activities of this kind can give strong expression to the comprehensive ideal, uniting students from very different backgrounds and providing a valuable source of support for disadvantaged students and those going through personal or domestic crises.

A sense of group identity of this kind can be particularly valuable in a large sixth form college where the comparative brevity of students' stay precludes the strong community feeling that many schools are able to engender. Fragmented programmes of study do not give academic students the same sense of belonging that many of their FE counterparts experience in following a coherent course taught by staff from one department. Many sixth form college students, of course, establish a strong allegiance to a component of their college experience: to one of their subject departments, to friendship groups, to particular staff, to extra-curricular activities such as sports teams, drama groups, orchestras and choirs. The tutor group, however, is a way of providing every single student with a point of reference: a physical base, a peer group that meets daily, a member of staff who has oversight of the students' total college experience.

Some comprehensive schools and sixth form colleges have designed a full programme of personal and social education for tutors to deliver in group tutorials. TVEE 16+ curriculum enhancement contracts have encouraged this development. These courses make considerable demands on staff, particularly on those tutors whose subject discipline affords them little or no experience of the subject matter of personal and social education or of the most appropriate methods of teaching this kind of course. There is a certain amount of staff resistance to structured group tutorials, not only from those who find the work difficult: confident tutors value the freedom to plan their own tutor group activities and to seize the opportunity of the moment or the topic that best suits their particular students. Thus, for various reasons, there is a tendency for structured tutorial programmes to be interpreted fairly freely and sometimes to be curtailed in favour of informal group activities that enable the tutor to undertake one-to-one counselling.

The latter is, of course, a very important part of the tutor's work and at times there are inevitably conflicting priorities between tutors' care responsibility for individual students and their work with the group as a whole. One can plan a year's course of groupwork, but not legislate for the uneven demands on tutors' time to meet students' counselling needs. At least one school – Medina High School on the Isle of Wight – has tried to solve this dilemma with a co-tutoring arrangement, two tutors being assigned to each tutor group. In group tutorials – allocated two and a half hours a week – one tutor undertakes the groupwork, while the other sees individual students.

There is general agreement among tutors that their counselling role has grown in significance and become more time-consuming. Tutors are becoming more involved in the processes of recording achievement, profiling and action-planning. At the same time, the more frequent incidence of broken homes, parental unemployment, house repossessions and reported child abuse have all increased the amount of casualty counselling required. Many personal or group tutors are undertaking the kind of counselling work previously associated with specialist FE and HE counsellors. Some undergo professional training for this work; the great majority, however, learn on the job, with support from occasional in-house staff development seminars and attendance at short courses. The more serious and difficult medical, psychological and personal problems are referred to specialists. Careers and higher education advice is given in-house by careers staff supported, in the past, by LEA careers officers. Some sixth form colleges have a department of careers staff, one of whom is a member of each team of tutors.

Much of the work that tutors do with individual students is undertaken in their own time and, as counselling demands have increased, tutors have tended to find less time for organising extra-curricular group activities. There is, too, a feeling in the colleges that students are less responsive than they were to staff-prompted social activities based on the institution's student groupings. Their preference is to organise their own activities through natural friendship groups or elected student committees. This accords with the trend in extra-curricular activities away from staff-run clubs and societies towards student-inspired initiatives. It may also be that, as the sixth form colleges grow in size and lose sight of their school origins, they are becoming less concerned about community spirit and group identity.

FE AND TERTIARY COLLEGE SYSTEMS

There is a different tradition of care and guidance in further education colleges. The coherence and vocational focus of most FE students' training programmes have given a departmental team of staff a natural overview of students' progress and career prospects. Thus these important aspects of support and guidance have been seen largely as a departmental responsibility.

Since the majority of FE students are adult or part-time members of college who attend no more than one day a week, lecturers have tended to confine their guidance to students' response to their course and prospective employment. It has not been a part of lecturers' responsibility to engage in activities aimed at character development or to offer advice on students' personal lives. That is not to say that individual lecturers have not become involved in such matters, but the institutional provision for the more personal care and welfare of students has traditionally been in the form of a trained counsellor or counsellors who are not part of the teaching staff. Students have been able to use the professional service these people provide and discuss in confidence any problems they are encountering in college or in their private lives. Where students' work, attendance or relationships appear to have been adversely affected by personal problems, staff have encouraged them to make contact with a counsellor. Counsellors normally work outside the departmental structure but a few colleges have a counsellor attached to each department.

The increase in the number of younger full-time students in FE has caused many colleges to question the adequacy of these arrangements which, in practice, depend largely on students' initiative and therefore place the emphasis on 'casualty counselling' - dealing with problems that are already well-established before they surface. The need for a more proactive system has been widely recognised, particularly for those students in the 16–19 group who are not the responsibility of any one department or identifiable course team.

GCE and GCSE students, and those whose vocational studies are made up of disparate components, are taught by a variety of staff who have no corporate identity and rarely any overall perception of individual students' total programmes of study. For these students, FE colleges have superimposed on their central counselling arrangements a system of personal or course tutors responsible for students' overall progress and general welfare. The staff who undertake this pastoral role have an allocation of about 15 to 18 students. Contact with students may be on an individual basis only, but more often they form an identifiable group which meets regularly with their personal or course tutor as in sixth form colleges and school sixth forms. This system has been more fully developed in tertiary colleges than in conventional FE establishments. The smaller tertiary colleges, in particular, have, from their inception, had a preponderance of full-time students aged 16–19 and have been particularly anxious to dispel a public perception that younger students are given less effective care and guidance in colleges catering for adult students than they are in schools and sixth form colleges.

In tertiary colleges all full-time students – academic and vocational – are normally assigned to a tutor group and a personal or course tutor. Thus nearly all full-time members of staff have a pastoral care role as well as a teaching responsibility. Vocational and academic students are often separated, the former being grouped on the basis of their course, the latter coming from different subject backgrounds. 'Academic' tutor groups may be loosely homogenous, with the tutor teaching everyone in the group for one main examination subject. In some colleges vocational and academic students are mixed. Students may be drawn from one year or be vertically grouped.

It is usual for tutors in a tertiary college to have a weekly tutorial with their groups, most commonly of an hour's duration but sometimes longer. This may simply be a way of ensuring access to students for individual counselling and guidance. Alternatively, it may be intended as a group activity in which the tutor delivers a personal development programme which includes careers/HE talks and guidance, health and sex education seminars and other general education components.

Tertiary college care and curricular management systems are often integrated, with personal and course tutors reporting to a director of studies or to faculty heads responsible for admissions and the negotiation of students' programmes of study. Alternatively, tutors' work is coordinated by a director of student services, either directly or via a tier of middle management. In both situations the tutorial system is linked to a student services team or support unit which provides a range of college-wide services – careers and higher education advice, counselling and medical help, student union activities and information services and facilities such as crèches and shops. One of the tutor's roles is to ensure that students requiring specialist help are aware of the opportunities available and the lines of communication to them.

The personal tutoring arrangements in the smaller tertiary colleges with a large intake of full-time students in the 16–19 age group are not dissimilar to those in sixth form colleges. Indeed, where tertiary colleges have evolved from sixth form colleges, they usually retain their former care system, perhaps with some minor modifications. In the larger colleges, where younger full-time students are still a minority, the *in loco parentis* role is sometimes taken less seriously.

RESOURCING THE CARE SYSTEM

Current care and guidance strategies make similar demands on accommodation to those relating to the academic and vocational curriculum. Personal development programmes with 16–19 students involve much group discussion and require appropriate seminar rooms or equivalent spaces: it is very difficult for even the most gifted tutor to run effective group tutorials in a traditional chemistry laboratory or engineering workshop. Ideally one-to-one counselling requires a small interviewing room or, at least, a recess in a larger teaching space.

The increased importance attached to the personal tutoring role, particularly in FE colleges, is one of several developments that have added to the complexity of teaching in recent years. The separation of the key management functions in schools and colleges means that staff belong to several teams and have a number of distinct areas of responsibility, often ranging across the curriculum, the care and guidance system, administration and the provision of resources. Whilst this situation clarifies roles and responsibilities, it increases the network of staff relationships and adds to the number of team and committee meetings that teachers have to attend. Conflicts of interest and priority can arise and, with several managers making demands and setting deadlines, workloads tend to increase.

Teaching has always been a demanding profession. The range of responsibilities that staff now have in addition to their classroom teaching requires a radical reappraisal of the administrative and resourcing support that they receive. FE colleges have long recognised the importance of relieving teaching staff of the extensive administrative routines associated with post-16 students and take for granted the need for a large team of ancillary staff that normally includes a registrar, examinations officer, qualified librarians and extensive departmental clerical and technical help. Schools and sixth form colleges have been constrained in this respect by an inability to vire their funds from one category of expenditure to another. That situation has now changed and in the next few years there is likely to be a considerable reallocation of administrative work in institutions with large numbers of post-16 students.

Chapter 10

Corporate colleges

THE NEW ROLE

The 1992 Further and Higher Education Act significantly changed the status of post-16 colleges by making them corporate bodies – freestanding, autonomous institutions responsible for their own affairs. As business organisations they have their own legal identity with the power to manage their assets and resources, employ staff, contract to provide services, engage in consultancies and join in cooperative enterprises with other companies. With a combined teaching and non-teaching staff of several hundred, and annual budgets of several million, the colleges fall into the category of medium-sized businesses. They have charitable status which enables them to benefit from donations, and exempts them from paying tax on earnings and rates on property. However, they cannot, as LEAs did, recover VAT payments.

With incorporation, college governors acquire the status of company directors and become subject to various Companies Acts that increase their responsibilities and accountability. They are given ultimate authority over colleges' general strategy, the curriculum, personnel management, student services and external relations. They can be held legally responsible if a college goes into insolvent liquidation and forced to make a personal financial contribution if it can be proved that they have failed to monitor their college's affairs properly.

Responsibility for maintaining the colleges was transferred under the Act from county and borough councils to central government or, in practical terms, from LEAs to two new government-appointed further education funding councils (one for England and one for Wales). These councils provide both capital funding for buildings and major items of equipment, and recurrent funding for running expenses. Allocations for major building projects are made on the basis of specific bids; those for equipment and minor capital works, such as repairs and adaptations, are decided on a formula basis. Recurrent funding comprises a cash limited block grant and a unit-funding payment based on the number of students on roll and the different categories and levels of work in which they are engaged. The student-related part of recurrent funding is weighted to provide a powerful incentive for expansion.

The funding councils have also assumed the strategic planning responsibility that LEAs formerly had for ensuring that adequate facilities exist for both full-time and part-time further education. Thus they advise the Secretary of State for Education on the need for additional colleges, mergers and closures. In fulfilling this role, the councils depend upon advice from regional advisory committees, which gather information on local needs and provision. These regional committees are expected to work closely with the Training and Enterprise Councils set up in 1989.

Incorporation has given colleges control of their own affairs and is intended to provide greater incentives and freedom to extend provision and increase student participation rates. Employers and politicians are agreed on the need for a major expansion of further education and training and the government sees the application of market forces to the 16+ sector as the best way of achieving this. The removal of the colleges from LEA control was also part of the government's determined policy to reduce the influence of the educational experts – advisers, inspectors, theorists – and to focus attention on pragmatic objectives. The colleges will become increasingly business-led, in their priorities, policies and management structures as well as in the composition and influence of their governing bodies.

THE FE RESPONSE

None of these developments came as a surprise to the world of further education. As long ago as 1963, the Robbins Report, although primarily concerned with higher education, recommended that detailed control of finances should go to FE colleges. Subsequently the view has been well canvassed that good management of the colleges has been 'inhibited by the excessive engagement in their affairs of local authorities exploiting their role as the formal employer of staff and the overseer of budgetary and purchasing matters' (National Advisory Body, 1987).

The colleges built up their own resistance to this situation and have, in recent years, tended to defer less and less to education officers and advisers, many of whom have not found it easy to keep pace with the non-curricular developments and increasing complexity of further education. This growing sense of independence has been encouraged by an increase in income from sources other than the LEA: fees from training contracts, short courses, consultancies and fee-paying students; Training and Enterprise Council money for Youth Training and Employment Training; funding from the Polytechnic and Colleges' Funding Council (PCFC) for higher education courses; and direct payments from HE institutions for franchise arrangements. In certain locations and socio-economic situations, the European Economic Community (EEC) is an additional provider of funds.

For a decade, FE colleges have been urged from all sides to be more entrepreneurial and enterprising in their efforts to increase student participation and to generate additional income. During the 1980s it was not sufficient for further education merely to be responsive to the changing needs of employers and students: there developed the concept of the proactive college which employs business methods to identify and target new client groups. During the same period, successive governments sought to hold down public expenditure whilst placing greater emphasis on efficiency and productivity. All these developments heightened awareness of the business side of college management and prepared the way for the changes that lay ahead.

The 1988 Education Reform Act required LEAs to delegate many of their responsibilities for running the FE and tertiary colleges to the institutions themselves. In particular, the colleges took control of their own budgets. Principals and senior staff had to develop a knowledge of the finer points of employment legislation and industrial relations which they had previously been able to leave largely to the LEA. At the same time, industrial and business representation on governing bodies was strengthened.

By the time that the government put forward its proposals for the new Further and Higher Education Bill in May 1991 (White Paper: *Education and Training for the 21st Century*), further education was alert to many of the implications of corporate status. Although LEAs fought a half-hearted rearguard action to retain their responsibilities, most were simultaneously engaged in a farewell liaison with their colleges to plan for a new era. By the beginning of 1992 some colleges had not only drawn up their corporate plans but put in place the structures and staff required to implement them. Nevertheless, Touche Ross, the management consultants contracted by the DES to guide colleges in their transition to incorporation, warned, in a report published in April 1992, that the majority of colleges had 'a lot to do' if they were to be ready for independence by the beginning of the financial year, 1993–94.

Most corporate plans consist of a three-to-five-year strategy taking colleges into the mid- to late-1990s. They are driven by the central requirements to expand provision and increase participation rates, particularly of full-time students in the 16–19 age range. Closer links are envisaged with partner schools, employers and higher education. More flexible entry requirements, course structures and timetabling arrangements are intended to widen access. Several colleges take the opportunity to review their equal opportunity policies and procedures relating to race, gender, disability and sexual orientation.

The corporate plans also address the challenge of the 1992 Act for colleges to raise standards and exercise effective quality control. Unequivocal assurances are given on such processes as target-setting, cost-effective course delivery, and review and evaluation procedures. The attitudes and pressures of the business world are rapidly becoming embedded in the colleges: objectives are more detailed and sharply focused, commitment to student-led curricula apparently wholehearted, and recognition of the need to comply with the paymaster's demands universal. A new language has been assimilated: educational aims have become *mission statements*, senior staff *managers*, principals *executives*. Frequent mention is made of *consumers*, *clients* and *customers*, although there is some uncertainty over precisely to whom such terms refer: students, employers or parents.

The corporate plans produced by the colleges are impressive documents matched only by the rhetoric of the prospectuses that articulate their mission to the public in general and prospective students in particular. As comparative newcomers to the market place, the colleges are inevitably talking up their ambitions and intentions. In so doing, they will need to bear in mind the dangers of widening the gap between rhetoric and reality all too common in the business world:

> in many companies vision or mission seems to be regarded as just 'words on paper'.
>
> (British Institute of Management, 1991)

Glossy prospectuses are no guarantee of quality in the service provided by education or business.

The new business functions recently acquired by the colleges have added substantially to their management tasks and the complexity of their organisational systems. New posts had already been created in response to the 1988 Education Reform Act in areas of marketing, public relations, finance, recruitment and income generation. Additional clerical and administrative appointments were made and many existing posts upgraded. Some major recruiters of fee-paying overseas students have employed specialist accommodation officers and additional student counsellors to look after their foreign students' special needs.

With the further appointments necessitated by the 1992 Act, whole new departments are now being created. Directors of finance, marketing and other business functions are being appointed at vice-principal level and thus afforded the same status as senior staff managing the curriculum and student services. The various responsibilities created or enhanced by incorporation are grouped differently in different colleges. Popular combinations are marketing and development, personnel and staff development, and finance/resources/management information systems. Marketing and development may be part of a larger 'client services' team which includes public relations and quality assurance.

A feature of the new senior appointments currently being made is that many have no qualifications or experience in education: they are accountants, personnel officers, publicity and marketing experts. As senior curricular and student services posts become vacant, replacements are being sought from those who have experience in industry or commerce as well as in education. The new generation of principals will have to possess, or quickly acquire, extensive business management skills. The scene is set for battles similar to those that are occasionally occurring over vice-chancellor/director appointments in higher education. With increased employer representation on college governing bodies, there will inevitably be appointing committees that split between those who see business expertise as the one essential prerequisite for a principal of a corporate college and those who remain convinced that credible leadership in education depends upon one's being able to understand and demonstrate the skills and qualities of the teachers one leads.

The concept of leadership has been out of favour for some time. However, at a time of radical new developments the need for clear direction, and therefore leadership, is once again crucial. Leadership and management are different concepts, albeit complementary and overlapping. Managers keep organisations running: they are concerned with the implementation of policy and the problems that people encounter in their day-to-day work; they control procedures, systems and equipment. Leadership involves a wider perspective: a clear perception of the total context and a vision of future direction. Organisations need leaders to enthuse, inspire and unite people in pursuit of a common purpose. Leaders set the agenda and build the team. They provide an example by their own contribution to the team effort and output. Senior staff within an organisation usually have both management and leadership roles, being responsible for an aspect of day-to-day organisation and implementation of policy, but leading teams in their own initiatives within agreed parameters. Management without leadership is mere administration.

At a time of exceptionally rapid development, leaders and managers are change agents who need to possess a wide range of process skills in research and planning, in problem-solving and decision-making, in motivating and communicating with people of all kinds within and outside the organisation. Increasingly these are qualities that businesses seek in the majority of their employees, not merely in their most senior staff. The old hierarchical systems are giving way to flatter, more flexible forms of organisation. More work is being undertaken in teams and an integrative approach adopted towards problem-solving. There are fewer functional specialists and departments, more need of multi-skills and people able to assume a range of responsibilities. Interdependence is replacing compartmentalisation. In these situations initial qualifications, length of experience, rank and position are becoming less important. The requirements are flexibility, adaptability and varied inter-personal and process skills.

Our educational system with its traditional overspecialised and content-based approach has not equipped people with the transferable skills and personal competences that are required in today's business world. Moreover, with some notable exceptions, business has not developed the understanding or training expertise needed to overcome these deficiencies. Corporate colleges bring the inadequacies of specialist education and training home to roost, for these colleges need the same wide-ranging staff skills as other businesses. The trend towards cross-college functions and varied staff roles is likely to continue and render irrelevant traditional line-management hierarchies. Moreover, questions are already being asked about the cost-effectiveness of top-heavy management structures with numerous highly-paid senior managers directing other people's output.

The East Birmingham College, an FE college with the equivalent of 3,000 full-time students, affords an example of a staffing structure which has dispensed with conventional line management. Although it retains the second-tier level of a line-management system, with four vice-principals responsible for students, operations, resources and development, the organisation is then flattened, with all full-time staff having significant teaching timetables and most taking some share in the college's management.

There are no faculties or departments. Sixteen programme area leaders are responsible for the delivery of courses. Staff are not grouped by courses but are a whole-college resource. Four quality improvement leaders support both academic and non-teaching staff in their efforts to improve the quality of the college's work. Another eleven staff have developmental responsibility for cross-college programmes in areas such as careers, HE access and equal opportunities. These staff are designated *programme leaders,* to demonstrate their equivalence to the *programme area leaders.* The college operates on fourteen sites each of which has a centre manager, paid on main grade lecturer level, responsible for resources. No member of staff holds more than one of these major responsibilities.

The large number of management roles means that many main grade lecturers carry what would normally be regarded as quite senior management responsibilities. There is financial recognition of this fact through a system of bonuses. The various teams are largely autonomous and run their own meetings: vice-principals have a supporting rather than directing or chairing role. Non-academic staff are organised into teams: there are none of the customary senior posts such as chief administrative officer and chief technician. The kind of trust normally placed in senior management is extended to all staff: there is no monitoring of their use of telephones or photocopying equipment, and all staff, teaching and non-teaching, are allowed computers at home on permanent loan.

The East Birmingham College concept is one of total quality management: staff have a high level of managerial responsibility and are accountable for their own work. The college is convinced that the system works – that there is a high level of staff commitment and a strong sense of collective momentum.

THE SIXTH FORM COLLEGE RESPONSE

The inclusion of sixth form colleges in the 1992 legislation that gave FE colleges corporate status had not been widely predicted. Over the last 25 years sixth form colleges have developed a distinctive form of 16–19 provision which has led them to lobby for the removal of inappropriate constraints imposed upon them by schools regulations, without necessarily seeking to come under further education regulations. In a developing situation the inflexibility of LEA categories of expenditure was particularly frustrating and the introduction of Local Management of Schools (LMS) in the 1988 Education Reform Act was especially welcomed by the sixth form colleges.

LMS was designed to give schools greater autonomy in managing their resources and to increase the proportion of LEA funding allocated on the basis of pupil numbers. Since its introduction, the extent of the delegation has been increased and the pupil-led funding principle strengthened. LEAs retain control of capital funds, central government grants and certain other items. They are, however, then required to pass on at least

85 per cent of their remaining funds to the schools and colleges, retaining only sufficient to discharge their statutory duties and to provide other essential LEA services.

Sixth form colleges were among the first institutions to be targeted by LEAs for LMS, and this gave them three years' experience of managing budgets before the full impact of incorporation in April 1993. Ostensibly, then, sixth form colleges' induction into business management was similar to that experienced by further education establishments. In reality, however, sixth form college principals and their senior staff faced a much steeper learning curve than their FE colleagues. Not only had the further education colleges experienced a degree of independence well before the 1988 Act, but they had always been more entrepreneurial and in tune with the business world than sixth form colleges. The bulk of their courses are specifically designed to meet employers' needs and entail close liaison with local firms. Many FE lecturers have worked in industry or commerce and understand the way business operates. They are generally more aware of the contractual aspects of their employment and are quite used to negotiating over such matters as overtime payments for additional work or time in lieu, something which, until recently, has been quite alien to schoolteachers.

Sixth form colleges belong to a different tradition. They evolved from grammar schools and most of their courses remain academic. The bulk of their staff come from an academic background, a considerable number having engaged in postgraduate studies or research. They are not, as a group, admirers of the enterprise culture and many are deeply suspicious of the concept of public services driven by market forces. This is generally true of the teaching profession as a whole and, even in further education, where business attitudes are more familiar, many lecturers are critical of the direction in which educational institutions are moving.

In their choice of career, teachers are influenced by different priorities from those that drive the business world. They are not strongly motivated by the pursuit of material wealth – either for themselves or as the daily objective of their working community. Through promotion and management responsibility some develop an interest in the financial aspects of educational management, but it has not, in the past, been something to which most teachers have given a great deal of attention.

One of the effects of the new legislation may be to change this situation. As the colleges become more and more business-led, the economic concerns of senior management will inevitably be reflected in internal systems and attitudes that affect all staff. One sees this in many higher education institutions where both departments and cross-institution services function like separate businesses, selling expertise and facilities not only to the outside world but to each other. Such an environment forces everyone to become cost-conscious. There is a heightened awareness of the need for good housekeeping and responsible financial control of public funds. There is also a tendency for income generation to become an overriding preoccupation so that everything one does is subconsciously, if not overtly, costed. Competition can become more important than cooperation and the community then loses any sense of coherence and unity.

Sixth form college staff have shown little enthusiasm for a set of externally-imposed reforms inspired largely by economic considerations. Their ideological objections have been matched by pragmatic concerns over job security, salary implications and uncertainty about conditions of employment. Principals have been rather more ambivalent and the official line of the Association of Principals of Sixth Form Colleges has been to welcome the opportunities offered by incorporation, whilst seeking reassurances over funding levels and mechanisms and establishing an employers' forum to determine salary structures should teachers' pay scales and conditions of service no longer be applicable.

Both sixth form and further education colleges were quick to foresee the dangers of plant bargaining over salaries. Although in the run-up to incorporation the principals settled for separate employers' organisations for sixth form and further education colleges, they agreed to work for convergence. However, the differences in tradition, size, function and philosophy make it unlikely that principals will ever speak with one voice.

Chapter 11

The future prospect

Recent government initiatives have removed the distinctions between colleges run under schools regulations and those belonging to the FE sector. All post-16 colleges now have incentives to develop both vocational and academic courses for students of all ages, including those wishing to attend part-time. Schools too are being encouraged to widen their provision by offering more vocational courses and by opening their doors to adults and part-time students. For the time being, most schools remain under LEA control, but the pace of opting out is increasing and it may not be very long before the great majority of secondary schools have joined the colleges as centrally-funded independent institutions.

LEA control of 16–19 provision sometimes acted as a brake on institutions' legitimate aspirations for development and growth, and this situation undoubtedly contributed to the authorities' undoing. However, LEA strategic planning of 16–19 education ensured a balance of courses in each region and established local systems and strategies that required schools and colleges to cooperate for the benefit of students.

The role of the LEA was crucial in the creation of sixth form college and tertiary college systems, in which schools have relinquished their sixth forms in favour of centralised 16–19 provision. Such schemes have done a great deal to widen the range of opportunities for post-16 students, particularly in areas where every institution has participated in the reorganisation. Whatever strategic planning role the further education funding councils develop, they are unlikely to expect cooperation on this scale from independent institutions keen to further their own interests. Indeed, existing cooperative systems are already under attack from a number of opted-out 11–16 comprehensive schools that have declared their intention to develop their own sixth forms in competition with local colleges. An increase in 16–19 educational providers, in areas where the age group's needs are already well-served, will be a retrograde step.

Another important feature of LEA control was the protection it afforded those institutions disadvantaged by their location, catchment area, accommodation, facilities, size or historical development. Schools and colleges operate in a variety of circumstances and the standards they achieve may be affected by numerous factors beyond their control. Without LEA support, some institutions are unlikely to survive for very long in the business world:

> The truth is, as history has so often shown us, that unfettered market forces lead to the rich and the strong growing richer and stronger and the poor and the weak poorer and weaker.
>
> (Edward Heath, 1985)

The theory behind incorporation is that competition will raise standards. In order to maintain their share of students, the less successful institutions will, it is argued, have to improve their reputation and therefore the quality of their provision as measured by published examination results.

In certain circumstances, the market mechanism can indeed lead to a general improvement in standards. If, for example, a particular manufacturer of domestic appliances, such as dishwashers, refrigerators and washing machines, increases sales at the expense of other companies, it may stimulate all its competitors to offer better value for money. Education, however, has different characteristics from domestic appliances. Moreover, colleges serve localities and compete for a limited number of students. Competition works better in some situations than others, and most economists consider market forces to be less effective in regional than national situations.

Without any restriction on their provision or sphere of operation, some corporate colleges will quickly attract more students. Others, for a variety of reasons not necessarily associated with the quality of the service they provide, will become less sought after. Once such differences manifest themselves, they will rapidly become self-perpetuating: the expanding colleges will attract additional resources for further development, whereas dwindling numbers and reduced funding will result in contraction and diminished choice for students in the less popular institutions.

With all providers of 16-19 education being encouraged to diversify their curricula and to increase access, the rhetoric suggests greater choice of courses and better matching of opportunities to meet individual student needs. The reality, however, is that the application of market forces to 16-19 education is likely to accentuate rather than reduce existing differences in the range and level of provision between institutions and regions. For many students, therefore, choice will be more limited than before. In the case of education

> the operation of the market is not marginal: it destroys choices for some as a result of others exercising choice. It cannot satisfy the basic condition of economic welfare, which insists that a change is categorically beneficial if everyone is either the same or better off.
>
> (Christopher Huhne, 1992:90)

The ability of colleges to heed the call to diversify will depend a good deal on their starting point. Sixth form colleges do not, at present, have the facilities to compete with Further Education across the full range of vocational courses. Where colleges previously run under schools regulations have successfully established a vocational curriculum, it tends to consist of first-level work for their less able students with perhaps some supporting courses for those studying A levels. The most popular courses are those leading to initial RSA and Pitman secretarial qualifications, first-level City and Guilds options and, since 1991, the BTEC First Diploma. Significantly, there has, in the past, been little interest in the higher level BTEC National Diploma, although this qualification has not been restricted to colleges run under FE regulations in the same way as the First Diploma. The core of sixth form college work is the academic curriculum and it is on this that the colleges' reputation and image are based.

Such is the demand for A level and GCSE courses, sixth form colleges often have difficulty in persuading students to undertake vocational alternatives, even when these are clearly more appropriate. The great majority of sixth form college applicants, strongly backed by their parents, are looking for the academic route to further qualifications. The problem for colleges wishing to develop higher level vocational work is thus twofold: they lack the appropriate facilities and resources, and they can rarely demonstrate the level of student demand to justify the capital outlay needed to overcome their deficiencies.

The staff of the newly designated corporate colleges are anticipating a period of considerable upheaval and uncertainty. Many of those in the smaller, less well equipped colleges feel that they may be threatened by takeover, merger or closure. Some observers suggest that the number of colleges will eventually be reduced from the 1992 total of more than 500 to as few as 200. Such forecasts are entirely speculative, but they do indicate the extent of the business failure that some educationists are expecting.

Many sixth form colleges are not only concerned about their comparatively poor base for developing an extensive vocational curriculum: they have strong reservations about the change of character and style that would accompany a new role as a multi-purpose college with large numbers of vocational, adult and part-time students. The sixth form colleges have always attached importance to the development of a strong community spirit and corporate identity, distinctive features made possible largely by the colleges' relatively small size and the homogeneous body of full-time students drawn from a narrow age band. Most of the colleges have also been able to achieve a very civilised atmosphere in which order and purposefulness combine with relaxed and friendly staff–student relationships.

There has already been some erosion of these qualities in the larger sixth form colleges, particularly where rapid growth has created overcrowding and problems of social control. The tertiary college experience indicates a very different environment when an institution is catering for several thousand full-time students on split sites and with large numbers of part-timers whose time in college is too short for them to develop any real allegiance or sense of belonging. Size brings benefits in terms of choice, flexibility and additional resources. The small sixth form college, however, may feel that there is a high price to pay for these advantages.

Assurances have been given that the sixth form colleges will not be forced into a precipitate change of role. However, the temptation of the extra funding that will accompany diversification and expansion may be irresistible, particularly if local circumstances suggest that the alternative fate could be takeover, merger or closure. Some colleges, however, may see a very different route to survival: through an intensification of the academic function and the distinctive sixth form college culture. The best way of competing in the market place is not necessarily to duplicate the full range of products or services offered by others, but often to specialise and to establish a reputation for things that others cannot or do not choose to provide. The response of some sixth form colleges to the invitation to diversify may be to establish a market niche by reverting to an earlier concept of the 16–19 college: the selective, A level institution.

In the short term, sixth form colleges keen to increase participation rates will no doubt select specific areas of potential growth, rather than attempt indiscriminate expansion. Some are already targeting the adult A level market, which would provide extra income without the need to design additional courses or provide new facilities. Smaller colleges, in particular, would benefit from increased enrolment on undersubscribed courses.

Development of a full evening programme to increase income and optimise the use of accommodation and equipment must be another popular strategy. Obvious starting points are the subject areas in which sixth form colleges have developed teaching strengths and facilities different from those of FE colleges. Some colleges will be well placed to challenge independent FE institutions in their favoured areas of the curriculum; for example, in the developing field of language teaching, not only foreign languages but English as a second and a foreign language and courses for prospective teachers of English to foreign students. Where colleges have very significant strengths they may consider recruiting beyond their traditional catchment area, even perhaps nationally and internationally. This of course raises the question of accommodation – boarding houses, hostels, lodgings – for students unable to travel daily.

Post-16 colleges are accustomed to competing for certain students, but this competition is certain to increase and there are already signs of growing suspicion between institutions. Colleges that have been LEA centres for specific specialisms will lose their exclusive right to a region's gifted students in a particular field such as music and drama and are likely to face competition where previously they enjoyed a monopoly. Under LEA direction or guidance, neighbouring sixth form and FE colleges usually agreed a certain amount of rationalisation of their provision, particularly where duplication would have been wasteful. This prevented institutions from undermining each other's courses and helped to keep relationships reasonably harmonious. Such agreements will require additional goodwill and regular renewal if they are to survive in future. The effort, however, would be worthwhile. TVEI liaison exercises have encouraged much profitable cooperation between sixth form and FE colleges: it would be a pity if this development were to become a casualty of incorporation.

The role of the school sixth form in the new pattern of 16–19 provision will be interesting. In the mid-1970s, with sixth form colleges and tertiary colleges developing apace, few commentators on the 16–19 scene doubted that the days of the maintained school sixth form were numbered. It has, however, survived, and the 1992 legislation effectively puts an end to a process of rationalisation that at one time seemed inevitable. A market-driven education service ensures variety, part of which is mixed school and college 16–19 provision.

At first glance, the school sixth form would appear to face great problems competing with the increasing range of opportunities available in the developing corporate colleges. Yet a trend towards very large tertiary-style institutions and an erosion of the distinctive features of the sixth form colleges could strengthen the appeal of the school sixth form to students and parents. The sixth form college and the smaller tertiary college have offered a compromise between the protective, familial school community and the more impersonal complex adult world of FE: a collegiate-style environment in which students can begin to exercise adult responsibilities whilst supported by a strong care and guidance system. Faced with a starker choice between a small school sixth form community and a multi-purpose college of several thousand, a sufficiently large number of students will choose the more personal, securer sixth form environment to ensure its survival.

Changed student attitudes will have a bearing on this situation. The present 16–19 age group has grown up in and been conditioned by the 1980s: more of its members are conservative, conformist and compliant than ten or fifteen years ago. Fewer are inclined to question the status quo, particularly if it can be seen to provide an effective route to further qualifications. This attitude inevitably helps a school to retain its older pupils. The school sixth form's acceptability is likely to be further enhanced if adults are seen to regard it as an appropriate environment for their continued education.

We inhabit a prosperous corner of the world and students expect to share in that prosperity. At the same time, high unemployment and pockets of obvious deprivation concentrate the mind on the constantly reiterated requirements for upward mobility: application, conformity and examination success. The public and grammar school sixth forms thrive in this climate. The combination of a selective intake and intensive tuition ensures examination success, parental satisfaction and an enviable public reputation.

Sixth form students are appreciative of the head start the public or grammar school gives them in the competition for more attractive careers and higher education places. Those who have friends and acquaintances in colleges and comprehensive schools may recognise that other environments offer a more liberal regime, less formal staff/student relationships and often more interesting syllabuses and study programmes. However, the prevailing attitude in the public and grammar school sixth form is that colleges and comprehensive schools have a *laissez-faire* attitude and do not make you work in the same way that selective schools do. Where students have yet to assume personal responsibility for their progress, 'being made to work' is naturally seen as a prerequisite for examination success and future preferment.

The sharply focused objectives of the public and grammar schools provide a clear sense of direction and purpose to all who work in them. Staff and pupils benefit from a stability and security sadly lacking in most comprehensive schools. Nevertheless, there is some staff unease that the nobler educational ideals can get lost in the single-minded pursuit of examination success. Senior staff in the more famous public schools, in particular, recall with a certain nostalgia the days when there were more important objectives in the sixth form than cramming for exams. The leisured class has, however, largely disappeared. The new clientele has different values and expectations and, from long experience of the business world, the public schools know that you provide what the customers pay for.

The country's most prestigious academic institutions – independent and maintained – are not expected to respond to the government's suggestion that sixth forms should diversify their curriculum to include vocational work. Moreover, a number of opted-out comprehensive schools have declared their intention to base their reputation on the academic standards of their sixth form. A situation in which an increasing number of sixth forms seek status and popularity by concentrating on academic work will have significant implications for LEA comprehensive schools developing their first-level vocational work. Too notable a success in the latter field could establish a sixth form's reputation for catering well for the less able, to the detriment of its A level course recruitment in competition with academic sixth forms. Fears of a two-tier state education system could prove well-founded in the 16–19 sector if right-wing advocacy of separate academic and vocational sixth forms were to become a reality.

Given the political nature of much educational change, it is tempting to speculate on how the 16–19 situation would have differed had a Labour government been returned in the 1992 general election. In terms of the pattern of provision, the answer is: probably not a great deal. Under Neil Kinnock's leadership, the Labour party in opposition largely conceded the utility of the free market and, some critics would say, in so doing denied the party's socialist principles and inspiration. Under a Labour government, Further Education colleges would have retained the corporate status newly conferred upon them by the 1992 Act, but with funding coming via LEAs instead of from a central funding council. Sixth form colleges would have been given the option of incorporation or LEA control. Opted-out schools would have been returned to LEAs but with the system of delegated budgets continuing. The balance of power would thus have been different and the move to incorporation slowed down. The trend, however, would have remained the same. Under such a mixed system and with a reduced Labour party commitment to state control, it is doubtful whether LEAs would have had the opportunity to continue with the kind of strategic planning and rationalisation of 16–19 provision undertaken in the period from 1966 to the late 1980s.

The area of immediate and significant change under a Labour government would have been the academic curriculum. Since 1988 the Labour party has espoused the recommendations of the

Higginson Committee for a more broadly-based programme of study and has also been influenced since 1991 by the more radical proposals from the Institute for Public Policy Research for a British Baccalaureate. A Labour government would no doubt have been quick to respond to the broad consensus that exists for 16–19 curricular reform.

Whether a Conservative government with a considerably reduced majority can hold out much longer against the curriculum reformers must be doubtful, particularly if one of its own departments, the DoE, continues to be such an effective catalyst for change. The establishment of separate vocational and academic sixth forms would of course help the government to keep Department of Employment and Department for Education influences apart and make it easier to pursue the present policy of promoting reform of the vocational curriculum whilst resisting changes to its academic counterpart. The college situation, however, looks like making this position increasingly untenable. Most corporate colleges will eventually adopt a tertiary style of provision with the greater opportunities that this affords to break down the artificial barriers between academic and vocational work.

Meanwhile, many of the developments that the government is resisting in the 16–19 sector – modularity, credit accumulation and transfer, flexible modes of course delivery and assessment, a much greater emphasis on understanding process and the acquisition of core skills – these are all gathering momentum in Higher Education, strongly supported by the DoE's Enterprise in Higher Education initiative. Moreover, the abolition of the binary divide at 18+ makes a nonsense of attempts to accentuate it at 16.

Such inconsistencies and contradictions are a feature of any system in transition, an inevitable consequence of change and uncertainty. They also reflect the conflicting aspirations of a society tempted by new world ideals whilst simultaneously clinging to the traditions of the past. The context in which teachers, lecturers and educational managers currently work is thus complex and frustrating. If this book has helped its readers in some way in their daily task of making local sense of national confusion, it will have served its primary purpose.

Bibliography

Advisory Council on Science and Technology (1991) *Science and Technology: Education and Employment*, London: HMSO.

Alexander, Sir William (1969) *Towards a New Education Act*, Cheam: Councils and Education Press.

Association of Principals of Sixth Form Colleges (1991) *A Framework for Growth: Improving the Post-16 Curriculum*, Wigan: APVIC.

Ball, Sir Christopher (1989) *Aim Higher: Widening Access to Higher Education*, London: RSA.

—— (1992) *Profitable Learning*, London: RSA.

Blair, T. and Straw, J. (1991) *Today's Education and Training: Tomorrow's Skills*, London: Labour Party.

Bolton School (1991) *Beyond the Fifth Form: A Guide for Parents and Boys*, Bolton: Bolton School.

British Institute of Management (1991) *The Flat Organisation: Philosophy and Practice*, Northampton: BIM.

Business and Technician Education Council (1991) *Common Skills*, London: BTEC.

Coldstream, P. (1989) 'How many graduates in the 21st century?' Director of the Council for Industry and Higher Education's Speech at the Institute of Manpower Studies, 11.89, London: IMS.

Confederation of British Industries (1989) *Towards a Skills Revolution*, London: CBI.

Consultants at Work (1990) *Managing Quality Improvement in Further Education: A Guide for Middle Managers*, Ware: Consultants at Work.

Cook, D. (1991) *College Principals' Responses to the White Paper*, Bristol: The Staff College.

Department of Education and Science (1957) Circular 323, *Liberal Education in Technical Colleges*, London: HMSO.

—— (1965) Circular 10/65, *The Organisation of Secondary Education*, London: HMSO.

—— (1984) *The Certificate of Pre-Vocational Education*, London: HMSO.

—— (1988a) *Education Reform Act*, London: HMSO.

—— (1988b) *Advancing A Levels*, London: HMSO.

—— (1989a) 'Further education: a new strategy', Secretary of State's Speech to ACFHE 2.89, London: DES.

—— (1989b) *Post-16 Education and Training: Core Skills*, London: DES.

—— (1990a) *Core Skills in Further Education*, London: DES.

—— (1990b) *Educational and Economic Activity of Young People Aged 16 to 18 Years in England from 1975 to 1989*, London: DES.

—— (1990c) 'Core skills for 16–19 year olds', Secretary of State's Letter to SEAC, 11.90, London: DES.

—— (1990d) 'A-levels', Secretary of State's Speech at Norwich School, 11.90, London: DES.

—— (1991a) *Education and Training for the Twenty-First Century*, Vols 1 and 2, London: HMSO.

—— (1991b) *Local Management of Schools: Circular 7/91*, London: DES.

—— (1991c) *Standards in Education 1989-90: The Annual Report of HM Senior Chief Inspector of Schools*, London: DES.

—— (1992) *Evaluating Developments in Advanced Supplementary Examinations 1990-91*, London: DES.

Department of Employment (1990) *1990s: The Skills Decade*, London: DoE.

Entwistle, N. (ed.) (1990) *Handbook of Educational Ideas and Practices*, London: Routledge.

Fullan, M. G. (1991) *The New Meaning of Educational Change*, London: Cassell.

Further Education Funding Council Unit (1992) *Preparing for Incorporation*, London: DES.

Further Education Unit (1989) *Towards a Framework for Curriculum Entitlement*, London: FEU.

—— (1990) *The Core Skills Initiative*, London: FEU.

—— (1991) *Flexible Colleges*, London: FEU.

—— (1992) *Core Skills in Action*, London: FEU.

Heath, E. (1985) 'North-south: the other common crisis', MP for Old Bexley and Sidcup's Speech to the Sunderland Conservative Association, 1.85, Sunderland: Conservative Association.

Huhne, C. (1992) *Real World Economics*, London: Penguin.

Independent Schools Information Service (1991) *Annual Census, 1991*, London: ISIS.

Institute for Public Policy Research (1990) *A British Baccalaureat: Ending the Division between Education and Training*, London: IPPR.

Institute of Manpower Studies (1989) *How Many Graduates in the 21st Century? The Choice is Yours*, London: IMS.

International Baccalaureate (1990) Bulletin No. 26, Geneva: IB.

James, F., Kershaw, N., Austin, M. and Miles, J. (1985) *Going Tertiary: A Commentary on Secondary–Tertiary Reorganisation*, London: TCA.

Jessup, G. (1990) *Common Learning Outcomes: Core Skills in A/AS Levels and NVQs*, London: NCVQ.

Joint Matriculation Board (1992) *General Certificate of Education Regulations and Syllabuses*, Manchester: JMB.

Lang, J. (1978) *City and Guilds of London Institute 1878-1978*, York: Ebor Press.

Ministry of Education (1957) *Circular 323: Liberal Education in Technical Colleges*, London: HMSO.

—— (1959) *Report of the Advisory Council for Education 15-18*, London: HMSO.

National Advisory Body (1987) *Management for a Purpose*, London: NAB.

National Commission on Education (1992) *Towards a Well Qualified Workforce*, London: National Commission on Education.

National Curriculum Council (1990a) *Core Skills 16-19*, York: NCC.

—— (1990b) *The Whole Curriculum*, York: NCC.

Oates, T. (1991) *Developing and Piloting the NCVQ Core Skills Units*, London: NCVQ.

Peterson, A. D. C. (1960) *Arts and Science Sides in the Sixth Form*, Oxford: OUDE.

Pilkington, P. (1991) *End Egalitarian Delusion: Different Education for Different Talents*, London: Centre for Policy Studies.

Post-16 Education Centre (1990) *News Issue No. 2: Post-16 Core and the Academic/Vocational Divide*, London: Institute of Education.

Rogers, A. (1986) *Teaching Adults*, Milton Keynes: Open University Press.

Royal Society (1991) *Beyond GCSE*, London: The Royal Society.

School Examinations and Assessment Council (1990a) *Consultation on the Draft Principles for GCE AS and A Examinations*, London: SEAC.

—— (1990b) *Examinations Post-16: Developments for the 1990s*, London: SEAC.

Schools Council (1969) *Working Paper 25: General Studies 16-18*, London: Evans/Methuen Educational.

Scottish Office Education Department (1992) *Upper Secondary Education in Scotland: Report of the Committee to Review Curriculum and Examinations in the Fifth and Sixth Years of Secondary Education in Scotland*, Edinburgh: HMSO.

Secondary Heads' Association (1989) *Planning 16-19 Education*, Bristol: SHA.

Smithers, A. and Robinson, P. (1989) *Increasing Participation in Higher Education*, Manchester: BP.

—— (1991) *Beyond Compulsory Schooling: A Numerical Picture*, London: Council for Industry and Higher Education.

Snow, C. P. (1959) *The Two Cultures and the Scientific Revolution*, New York: CUP.

Spours, K. (1989) *Promoting Progression: Prospects for a Post-Sixteen Modular Framework*, London: Institute of Education.

Standing Conference of Tertiary and Sixth Form College Principals (1990) *Compendium of Tertiary and Sixth Form Colleges*, Southport: SCOTVIC.

Taylor, I. R. (1989) *School Industry Linked Projects: Experiential*

Group Work, An Evaluation Report, Liverpool: University of Liverpool.

Toogood, P. (ed.) (1991) *Governing Colleges into the Twenty-First Century*, Bristol: The Staff College.

Touche Ross (1992) *Getting Your College Ready: A Handbook of Guidance*, London: HMSO.

Wearing King, R. (1968) *The English Sixth-Form College*, London: Pergamon Press.

Welsh Joint Education Committee (1991) *GCE–GCSE 1991 Syllabuses*, Cardiff: WJEC.

Wragg, E. (1991) 'Coming of age', *Times Educational Supplement*, 3904, 21–2, London: TES.

Index